An Anthropologist Looks at History

A. L. KROEBER

AN ANTHROPOLOGIST LOOKS AT HISTORY

With a Foreword by MILTON SINGER

Edited by THEODORA KROEBER

UNIVERSITY OF CALIFORNIA PRESS
1963   Berkeley and Los Angeles

UNIVERSITY OF CALIFORNIA PRESS
BERKELEY AND LOS ANGELES

CAMBRIDGE UNIVERSITY PRESS
LONDON, ENGLAND

© 1963 BY THE REGENTS OF THE UNIVERSITY OF CALIFORNIA
LIBRARY OF CONGRESS CATALOG CARD NO.: 63-16250

FOREWORD

Modern anthropology offers to the study of the cultural history of civilizations two important insights: (1) that every culture is a complex and composite growth which derives most of its component elements from its own past or has borrowed them from other cultures; and (2) that every culture tends to develop a distinctive organization, coherent and self-consistent, which tends to absorb new elements, whether borrowed or indigenous, and to reshape them to accord with its own patterns. At first sight these two insights seem to be in conflict or at least divergent. For the first leads to the long-run telescopic view of culture as a collection of elements, such as the plow or the alphabet, spreading around the world to combine and recombine in the mosaics of history. The second leads by contrast to the more subjective and short-run apprehension of coherent and meaningful patterns, values, and ways of living in local cultural growth.

Alfred Kroeber has shown us, perhaps more clearly than any other anthropologist, that those two insights are not in opposition but are complementary and can be combined. He has done this first by bringing all of human culture into view with his magnificent high-powered telescope, and then by tracing the growth patterns of those large, literate cultures called civilizations. He has not hesitated to use whatever help he could get from archaeology and prehistory; periodic, general, and regional history, and ethnography and ethnology. At the same time, he has taken pains to emphasize that the recognition and description of culture patterns is different from the recording and narration of events. The pattern approach requires discernment of the shadowy, groping beginnings of the selective commitments to particular styles, especially in intellectual and esthetic activities, and then the observation of how progressive mastery is achieved, the potentialities of the styles realized, and new styles developed. The resulting description is in terms of a series of profiles of culture growths. Where a number of these series are contemporaneous or overlap in one geographical area and tend to mutual consistency, we have, says Kroeber, the style nexus or total culture pattern of a whole culture or civilization.

The growth profiles of civilizations do not follow a uniform birth and death cycle, as Spengler held, but show pulsating rhythms, with peaks of growth which tend to cluster during relatively brief periods of a civilization's history. Kroeber calls these peaks "culminations" or "climaxes" of whole culture growth, and amply documents their existence in his book *Configurations of Culture Growth*.

It is noteworthy that he developed this concept of "climax" when he was finishing his book *Cultural and Natural Areas of Native North America*, just before he turned to a serious study of civilizations. His theory of civilization is thus continuous with his theory of preliterate cultures and his work on archaeology. The findings of the *Configurations of Culture Growth* in any case give support to the general conclusions of the *Culture Areas* study on the relations of growth culminations to degree and intensity of organization of culture content: namely, that the growth peak of a civilization tends to coincide with a period of successful organization of culture content—that is, the organization of ideas, styles, and standards. Kroeber sees cultural creativity and assimilation running ahead of organization before the culmination, and running behind it after, as the organization tends more and more to repetition and rigidity.

A corollary of this relation between culmination and cultural organization may be of considerable importance for understanding processes of modernization and culture change: as a culture becomes richer in number of elements, it also tends to become more highly organized, and this tends to increase its capacity to assimilate more elements, whether produced by itself or borrowed from without. This means that successful absorption should lead to greater inventiveness and productiveness.

Why this process should fail in any particular case, and decline should set in, is not yet clear. Kroeber was more interested in the what and how of the process than in the why. He did not rule out causality for the rise and decline of cultures and civilizations, but he thought it very difficult to determine causes. From his long-run view, the bulk of impinging causality was below the surface of the present, because most of a group's culture is a product not of the living population but of its preceding generations, and the majority of the content of any culture has normally been produced by other groups and introduced and accepted. We must agree with him when he writes that "with ancient and recent, outside and internal factors all at work and of an indefinitely great variety of ages and proveniences, it is easy to see why the causality of cultures, viewed historically, should be both intricate and diffuse." [1]

Kroeber was of course aware of the adaptiveness of culture growths to environmental and other circumstances, particularly in the fields of subsistence and of social and political organization. He was more interested, however, in the bursts of cultural creativity and development whose shaping "forces" were cultural patterns and styles. About the causes of these patterns and styles he was not willing to speculate, beyond noting the historical contexts of the occurrence of the patterns and insisting that the causes must also be in cultural phenomena, in other patterns and styles, and possibly in the pulsings of "free" human energy and strivings.

It is ironic that his caution on questions of causality should have evoked the criticism that Kroeber's theory of culture leads to a culture and pattern determinism. In fact Kroeber has admitted

---
[1] Kroeber, *The Nature of Culture* (Chicago, University of Chicago Press, 1952), Introduction.

that in his earlier writings he himself used deterministic language, which he abandoned in his later writings. Three features of his theory of culture contribute to an impression of determinism: (1) Because culture patterns abstract from the events of history and from the concrete acts of particular individuals, the impression arises that individuals and their choices and actions do not count. (2) This impression is reinforced by the fact that, in the long view of history which Kroeber takes, particular individuals are rarely visible or known. (3) Finally, the descriptions of patterns are apt to be read as *laws* of general application.

Some of these impressions are misleading. The patterns are not deterministic laws but more or less definite ways of acting, thinking, doing things, developed by people who, as they become conscious of them, may acquire great skill and mastery in evolving and controlling the patterns. Culture patterns do not occur in the absence of human beings; on the contrary, Kroeber believed that only human beings produce culture, while other animals may have society. Once culture has been produced by human beings, however, he thought it could be studied legitimately and fruitfully in abstraction from particular individuals.

Kroeber's theory of culture does not necessarily imply any strict determinism or causality, cultural or otherwise. His "repression" of individuals is strictly methodological, a deliberate effort to hold constant the psychological and other non-cultural factors, while he studied the quality and sequences of cultural forms. The relations of these forms to individual personality, to social structure and organization, and to many other factors, were problems to be investigated by others, with different methods and concepts. When some of these other kinds of studies were developed in social anthropology and in personality and culture studies, Kroeber acknowledged that they added depth to the descriptions of culture patterns. In the essay "On Human Nature," he sketches a program of research that would federate biological, psychological, social, and cultural levels. In several earlier writings also he attempted personality characterizations of areas and cultures. His ventures into these fields came only *after* he felt that the autonomy of the study of culture had been won and established.

Kroeber's conscious and single-minded separation of the cultural aspects of phenomena from the non-cultural was justified by the results. In the study of civilizations, it led Kroeber to illuminate many problems and processes—the problems, for example, of the delimitation of civilizations, their distinctiveness, internal consistency, continuities and discontinuities. These have not yielded much to the normal methods of historians or of anthropologists. Kroeber's approach to these problems, in terms of style patterns, their growth, clustering culminations, decline, reconstitution, and disintegration, has given us the beginnings of an understanding of the rise and decline of civilizations; not as a product of race, environment, or great men, but as a phenomenon of cultural creativity. The method has also led Kroeber to investigate how the civilizations of Asia, Europe, Africa, and America are interrelated in purely cultural terms.

In the discussion of Kroeber's paper "History and Anthropology in the Study of Civilizations" at the Behavioral Sciences Center Seminar in 1958, Robert Redfield, noting that Kroeber's conception of a comparative study of civilizations as a history of all human cultures and their interrelations excluded social anthropology, asked whether there could also be a social anthropology of civilizations, of their morphology and genetics. Kroeber replied that he would not deny such a possibility, but that the social anthropology of the last decade took a microscopic view dealing only with short-run change, whereas he had been talking about a telescopic view. When Redfield suggested the possibility of extending social anthropology to a macroscopic natural history of civilizations, Kroeber said he would guess that social anthropology is more likely to find a microscopic physiology than a macroscopic morphology.

What Redfield had in mind, and had to an extent presented at the seminar, was the possibility of studying and comparing civilizations as structures and social organizations of traditions, little and great. It was clear from this interchange that, while Kroeber did not wish to discourage anyone from such a study, he himself was sceptical about its outcome. This scepticism probably derives from his view, expressed in a number of places in the present essays, that social anthropology, community and acculturation studies, and even ethnographic studies of primitive cultures, lack a genuine historical approach and are apt to get lost in microscopic analyses of a few local societies or cultures without wide significance. Undoubtedly, the microscopic, synchronic study has been the dominant trend in social anthropology, but there has also been a minority trend which takes history seriously and which seeks broad comparisons. Redfield on peasant societies and cultures, Eggan on the historical changes of types of kinship systems, Spicer on the acculturation history of the Southwest Indians, and the recent series of restudies by Redfield, Lewis, Mead, Firth, and others, show an increasing concern among social anthropologists with the problems of an historical approach and with cultural processes that may also be significant in the history of civilizations.[2] To be sure, the range of history usually covered in these studies is still quite short by comparison with the history of all

[2] Robert Redfield, *Peasant Society and Culture: An Anthropological Approach to Civilization* (Chicago, University of Chicago Press, 1956); Fred Eggan, "The Cheyenne and Arapaho System," *Social Anthropology of North American Tribes* (Chicago, University of Chicago Press, 1937), "Historical Changes in the Choctaw Kinship System," *American Anthropologist*, XXXIX, No. 1 (1937), 34–52, "Social Anthropology: Methods and Results," *Social Anthropology of North American Tribes* (2d ed., 1955), pp. 485–551; Edward Spicer, *Cycles of Conquest* (Tucson, University of Arizona Press, 1963), and Spicer (ed.), *Perspectives in American Indian Culture Change* (Chicago, University of Chicago Press, 1961); Redfield, *A Village that Chose Progress: Chan Kom Revisited.* (Chicago, University of Chicago Press, 1950); Oscar Lewis, *Life in a Mexican Village: Tepoztlan Restudied* (Urbana, University of Illinois Press, 1951); Margaret Mead, *New Lives for Old; Cultural Transformation—Manus, 1928–1953* (New York, Morrow, 1956); Raymond Firth, *Social Changes in Tikopia: Restudy of a Polynesian Community after a Generation* (New York, Macmillan, 1959). Among British social anthropologists Evans-Pritchard has stressed the historical approach in "Social Anthropology: Past and Present," *Man* (1950), and in *Anthropology and History* (Manchester, Manchester University Press, 1961).

FOREWORD   xi

human culture. On the other hand, these studies show a flexibility in social anthropology as to method and concept that may yet lead it to join with Kroeber's culture history for a coöperative study of an anthropology of civilizations.

Kroeber's comments on "Holism and World View" show his willingness to think about and explore Redfield's suggestion of a social anthropology of civilizations, although he believed that civilizations were too massive for a "functional" dissection of their inner connections.[3] These comments also illustrate one of Kroeber's most characteristic gifts as a natural historian of culture: the ability to take in a large corpus of complex material and to distill the essentials from it in an orderly and concise manner. At the Palo Alto Seminar on comparative civilizations, after he had been listening to presentations by Robert Redfield, Arthur Wright, Gustave von Grunebaum, Nirmal Kumar Bose, Ethel Albert, and Charles Wagley, dealing with problems of holistic characterization in different cultures and civilizations, he was stimulated to bring in to the seminar for discussion the very compact summary and analysis which appears as Paper Number 7.[4] The seminar accepted Kroeber's summary with one or two minor qualifications. It is easy to see why Kroeber should have found the approaches he summarizes congenial to his own approach to the study of civilizations, for that also is holistic, comparative, and intuitive. He also finds in the discussion of "world view," "self-image," and "ideal pattern" a link between the insider's collective self-view and the anthropologist's recognition of culture pattern. If I were to put

---

[3] Kroeber, *A Roster of Civilizations and Culture* (New York, Viking Fund Publications in Anthropology, No. 33 (1962), p. 15.

[4] Some of these presentations have since been published: Robert Redfield, "Civilizations as Things Thought About," "Civilizations as Social Structure," and "Civilizations as Cultural Structure," in *Human Nature and the Study of Society: Papers of Robert Redfield*, Vol. I (Chicago, University of Chicago Press, 1962). Arthur Wright, "The Study of Chinese Civilization," *The Journal of the History of Ideas*, XXI (1960), G. E. von Grunebaum, "An Analysis of Islamic Civilization and Cultural Anthropology," *Modern Islam: The Search for Cultural Identity* (Berkeley and Los Angeles, University of California Press, 1962).

Kroeber's subtle intimations into bold and explicit terms, the summary would run something like this:

There is a continuum of cultural and societal wholes ranging from the little traditions and little communities of isolated primitive tribes to nations, civilizations, regional culture areas and oikumenés. To the natural historian of culture and society all segments of the continuum deserve serious study, even the "footnote cultures," which correspond to the lamprey in biology. In varying degree, members of all cultures and societies recognize the coherence and distinctiveness of their own culture and give it articulate formulation, through the activities of specialists, in a self-image and a world view. Although self-image and world view are idealizations which distort reality, they are nevertheless creative fictions which may impose their influence on all parts of a culture. In the case of nonliterate, primitive societies, where little is known of the world beyond one's own culture and society, self-image and world view coincide. In literate cultures, however, and particularly in the modern West, where recognition of reality tends to increase, as science expands knowledge of the world, self-image and world view no longer coincide. Some contact with, and relative isolation from, other cultures is probably a condition for the formation of a sense of cultural identity that is distinctive and contrastive to other cultures. The increase in intensity of intercultural contacts that comes with westernization and modernization may destroy the needed "protective isolation" and thus break down the regional differentiation of the world's cultures. If this happens, distinctive cultural self-images and world views may still continue but they will be differentiated by time periods rather than by the regional area where they took root.

I do not think that in these hypothetical suggestions Kroeber is merely letting his imagination go. He is thinking about long-run trends in cultural development which are wholly consistent with his studies of past development. The decreasing influence of environment on cultural development is one of these trends which he has noted in the history of the native cultures of North America as well as in the history of the Old World civilizations.

He has also noted long-run uniformizing and unifying trends in many spheres of culture. The major civilizations, he frequently observes, are all supranational and multilingual; cultural internationalism precedes political internationalism.

On the other hand, Kroeber did not see the future of civilization and culture as simply following the main trends laid down in the past. At the end of the essay on "Periodization," he suggests several important reasons why the natural history of civilizations and their stylistic organization may be quite different in the future from what they were in the past. Modern man, with his rapid means of communication, has within his reach an "international pool of styles" upon which to draw. He no longer is under the dominance of one style at a time. This is as true of styles of science as of styles of art. Under these conditions, moreover, gifted individuals may be able to originate a number of different styles in a single lifetime. Kroeber cites Picasso as an example of this possibility, which he regards as "an indubitably new phenomenon and perhaps a precursor of more to come."

Gerald Holton, a physicist at Harvard, has published a study of recent scientific growth which graphically supports Kroeber's observations on the acceleration and internationalization of styles in scientific thought and research.[5] Robert Oppenheimer, as well, reflecting on similar trends, has pointed out that science as a specialized cultural tradition owes its development to contributors of whom 93 per cent are still living.[6]

The acceleration in the development and spread of styles in art and in science may not extend to all other spheres of culture. In science itself, the stylistic innovations tend to get stabilized by a cumulative irreversible direction of growth. Nevertheless, the vigorous creativity in these major intellectual and esthetic spheres of civilization does begin to show a pattern of cultural growth and diffusion different from the past. In the past, cultural styles and organizational patterns were slow to change and spread, as

---

[5] Gerald Holton, "Scientific Research and Scholarship, Notes toward the Design of Proper Scales," *Daedalus* (Spring, 1962).
[6] Oppenheimer, *Encounter* (October, 1962).

Kroeber pointed out in his 1923 edition of *Anthropology* (pp. 130–131). They developed through a slow process which included the social inheritance and acceptance of borrowed cultural elements and the adapting of these borrowings to environmental and societal requirements, as well as the play of imaginative and intellectual energies. The interflow among cultures and civilizations was a flow and fusion of culture elements, not of culture styles or patterns of cultural organization.

Now we see, with the help of Alfred Kroeber's more recent insights, that cultural styles, patterns, and ways of life may also change, interpenetrate, and diffuse as they are freed from their ancient moorings and are taken under sail by the pilots of present and future generations. In this new change lies both the hope and the predicament of modern man as he looks for a cultural identity which will give direction and destination to his voyage.

June 11, 1963   MILTON SINGER

CONTENTS

INTRODUCTION — xvi
PART ONE
1. The Delimitation of Civilizations — 3
2. Have Civilizations a Life History? — 18
3. The Time Profile of Western Civilization — 28
4. Flow and Reconstitution within Civilizations — 39
5. Periodization — 60
6. The Role of Style in Comparative Civilizations — 66
7. Holism and World View — 90

PART TWO
8. Integration of the Knowledge of Man — 101
9. What Ethnography Is — 131
10. An Anthropologist Looks at History — 152
11. History and Anthropology in the Study of Civilizations — 160
12. The Personality of Anthropology — 172
13. Evolution, History, and Culture — 179
14. On Human Nature — 200

INTRODUCTION

An Anthropologist Looks at History is a collection of papers from Alfred Kroeber's writings during the last decade of his life. Five of them were in completed manuscript form and are here published for the first time. In all of them, Kroeber is looking, prodding, speculating, on *style*, on *civilizations*, on *history*, on the place of anthropology in the world of scholarship and in the family of man.

In a sense the book enforced itself, its materials flowing away from the linguistic, critical and substantive ethnology Kroeber did during the same decade, and gathering themselves together under one of his own titles as will be seen, paper 10 of this volume.

But there was further reason for this selection: Milton Singer and I, who made and ordered the selection, have in mind the traditionally trained but original young scholars who are beginning to make themselves felt intellectually in the history of science and the history of ideas. They keep a lookout for clues to a particular aspect or trend which will lead them farther into their subject and to ultimate understanding of its many and complex aspects and trends. And anthropology, as a young and growing science with old philosophical roots in the past and a world view all its own, is of central interest to some of these young scholars.

We have in mind also the graduate student of anthropology

INTRODUCTION

who presently enters the profession at a moment when its prevailing climate happens to be non-historical. We offer him a brief view of the aspect now in shadow that he may be prepared—pleasurably or apprehensively, depending upon his bent—to see the historical face of his subject again swing into full light.

We hope that title and subject matter commend themselves to the critical attention of historians; and it is the intent of our presentation as it was Kroeber's own attitude that it is he and anthropology which are honored in the association.

We place in time and circumstance each of the unpublished papers, all of them but one having been read by Kroeber to an audience for whom they were particularly written.

For those readers who did not know Kroeber as person or teacher, it becomes our task to place him somewhat as scholar and person in the perspective of anthropology today. To this task I can contribute only my own personal understanding of that part of his work which seems to me to have been directly ancestral to the content of this book.

It is true of the papers here, as of much of Kroeber's writing, that their materials are of interest to non-anthropologists. They can be said to be anthropological, some of them, principally in the sense that no one but an anthropologist would have so formulated them: they exemplify Kroeber's individual "pattern" and "style." He was, as person and anthropologist, remarkably "of a piece," his earliest interests and his earliest writings previsioning the later man and work, or so others have said of him. He came gradually to handle larger congeries of material with ever greater skill and ease as he became older: in his seventies and eighties he was still deepening and furthering and defining the pattern. The whole development cannot be gone into here, but to understand it somewhat as it appears in this book, it is sufficient to go back only so far as an undergraduate course called "Culture Growth" which Kroeber offered first in 1921 and thereafter, each year he was in residence at the University of California, Berkeley, through 1945.

Unlike other courses in anthropology which were molded and remade by many hands, many voices, the name, content, and presentation of "Culture Growth" was Kroeber's own. When he was away, it was not offered. It remained his favorite undergraduate course; was not required of majors in anthropology; and drew heavily from students in the physical and natural sciences and the humanities, for many of whom it was their only course in the subject. They did well for the most part and enjoyed the flying journey on which Kroeber took them back into remote prehistory and on up to the recent past; nor did anyone mind that he had a way of ending short of the announced destination, having loitered along one pleasant bypath and another en route.

I urged him to put this liveliest of courses into a book. He said no, it would then be dead, tied to its tracks. "I will write it when I am retired," he said. But he did not write it. *A Roster of Civilizations* was to have been its mature summation.

Immediately ancestral to the materials of this book is Kroeber's *Configurations of Culture Growth*. Of this book, I particularly recall the seven prewar years when every summer, every holiday and free hour went into the tasks of research, thinking through and writing it. Never much liking theory for its own sake, Kroeber found a way of organizing units of concrete data into theoretically meaningful and manageable complexes. *Configurations* was published in 1944, having been delayed by the war. In 1945 Kroeber delivered the Huxley Memorial Lecture for that year before the Royal Anthropological Society in London—"The Ancient Oikoumenê as an Historical Culture Aggregate"—which grew out of *Configurations* as the papers and books of the 1950's would take their rise in the *Oikoumenê*.

When *Configurations* was at last behind him, Kroeber came out literally on the sunny side of it, somehow free at last as he had not felt free before, to add his sensibility to form, styles, values, and aesthetic truths to his other approaches to the always fascinating phenomena of culture. This sensibility should have been given fuller expression in a book on the arts. There are hints in some of the papers here as to the probable range and style of the book had Kroeber written it, the best single exemplar being the brief paper "Periodization." He did not write a book on the arts, in part no doubt because for the fifteen years following his retirement he was in temporary residence in as many places, and one needs one's own library for such a work; in part because linguistics consumed such great blocks of his time during those years; but in large part, I fear, because his children and I lured him into talking with us about art and artists, about theories of creativity and of beauty, about everything which might have gone into the book. These conversations were restful and fun for him and exciting for us, but now we feel some sense of guilt at our selfishness.

The anthropologist today goes to India and Africa as handily as Kroeber once went up the creeks and into the hills of California; governments call on him and occasionally listen to his advice; between times, he participates in the hypothesized thinking of today's intellectuals. He has today, as in the past, the excitement of new fields, new styles, new formulations and solutions.

Perhaps he too will find himself returning in twenty or forty or sixty years to an inner center as aesthetically and anthropologically meaningful to him as culture was to Kroeber—the great human and humane achievement as he understood it—modern man's faith and hope for his own and his species' future.

February, 1963   THEODORA KROEBER

PART ONE

The papers of Part One all have to do with ways of knowing and comparing civilizations. Their ultimate goal might well be called an anthropology of civilizations, although Kroeber used no such highfalutin phrase to described what he sought.

The first five papers suggest each, one way of making comparisons between civilizations.

Paper 4 which is called "Flow and Reconstitution within Civilizations," was read by Kroeber at a dinner meeting at the Wenner-Gren Foundation in New York City in 1958, under the title, "Reversibility." Its present fuller title is more accurately descriptive of the contents in its present full form and will, it is hoped, alert the reader to what Kroeber was doing, which was to demonstrate applications of relatively dense historiographical theory to familiar examples from history.

Paper 5, titled here "Periodization," was with others of Kroeber's unpublished pieces, but without direct relation to them, and unlike the others, it had not been given a title. Although it seems to be essentially notes for a later full treatment, it is included here because it makes some points not elsewhere touched upon.

In the spring of 1958, at the Center for Advanced Study in the Behavioral Sciences at Stanford, California, Milton Singer and David Mandelbaum chaired a symposium on "Comparative Civilizations" with afternoon meetings two or three times a week for eight weeks. Papers were presented orally but with the core text for the day nonetheless thoroughly thought through and in writing. The discussion was varied and informed, the symposium participants being themselves culture historians of one sort or another.

"The Role of Style in the Study of Comparative Civilizations," paper 6 of this book, was one of Kroeber's formal contributions to the symposium, printed here for the first time and differing somewhat from his customary "written" style. Beginning with the point of view and materials of his then recently published book, *Style and Civilizations*, it is soon following new leads suggested by the discussion and interests of the other symposium members, and it indicates Kroeber's own continuing beguilement with the role of style in culture.

The last paper of Part One, "Holism and World View" is from the same symposium on comparative civilizations. It is little more than a sketch, lively and germinal.

The reader will observe that there are repetitions in some of the papers of the explanation of the points of view of the writers, Oswald Spengler and Arnold Toynbee. Kroeber would have removed these had he juxtaposed the papers as we have in this book. I considered doing so, but decided against it: the papers were read to audiences not all of whom could be assumed to be familiar with these writers; and in each instance of repetition, Kroeber's angle of approach or emphasis is special. Those readers who know the Spengler and Toynbee interpretations, particularly of the civilizations of China, will skim past the explanations of them here. I did not interpret my function as editor to be that of cutting or rewriting.

1. The Delimitation of Civilizations

THE PROBLEM of the delimitation of civilizations is one which the work of historians projects but hardly attempts to solve. Once the historic courses of civilizations have been traced, comparison between them becomes an obvious interest. Reference is not to any philosophy of history aiming to string civilizations like beads on the thread of some pervasive principle, but to a pragmatic or empirical approach such as sociologists or anthropologists are accustomed to use. Most common, because most practicable in such researches, are comparisons limited to segments of civilization —to the family, state, religion, economy, or even oftener to particular institutions or practices within these.

Nevertheless it is inevitable that sooner or later systematic comparison should be extended to civilizations as wholes. The works of Danilevsky, Spengler, and Toynbee are examples. Toynbee seems to be the only historian who has committed himself outrightly to the endeavor. He not only enumerates and defines his civilizations, but states the criteria by which he defines them. He is therefore conscious of the problem of delimitation of civilizations to a much greater degree than most anthropologists and sociologists who tend to take civilizations for granted. He is also more conscious than are most historians, who in general touch the problem only tangentially, because customarily they operate within the limits of a single civilization rather than interculturally.

Reprinted by permission from *Journal of the History of Ideas*, Vol. XIV, No. 2 (April, 1953), 264-275.

Toynbee's premise, that certain significances of history become apparent only on a supernational, total-civilizational view, leads first to focussing on culture wholes, and then to their comparison. And he admits that the units that are to be compared need to be defined by standardized criteria.

Now, anthropologists have long been accustomed to describe whole cultures. But these have belonged to small societies of tribal size, unlettered, and hence without a recorded history of their own. Ethnographic accounts are usually based not on search and exploitation of already extant documents, but on newly made documents resulting from face-to-face interviews and observations. While fundamentally the two groups aim at fairly parallel objectives, anthropologists can be roughly compared to reporters, historians to rewrite men or editors.

But in spite of their interest in "culture wholes," anthropologists have shown marked reluctance to concern themselves with the larger culture wholes ordinarily called civilizations. In part this is due to inexperience in dealing with documentary records. But since it remains theoretically feasible to attempt non-archival, synchronic, cross-sectional analyses and syntheses of national and supernational civilizations, on the precedent of those which anthropologists are accustomed to make for tribal cultures, it is evident that the mere size of the subject also tends to act as a deterrent to anthropologists. Instead, their tendency has been to do community studies, where the size and scope of investigation are convenient and familiar. In such community studies the unit dealt with is not self-sufficient. It constitutes so to speak but a cell or at most an organ instead of an autonomous whole. By contrast, when anthropological endeavors have taken on broader scope, they have inclined to lack depth and factual substantiality, remaining spotty or impressionistic and concerned with considerations like national character or ethos. Clearly, neither of these approaches is likely to face the problem of what delimits a major civilization.

This problem of delimitation does have a fair parallel in historical biology—what is conventionally called evolutionary or systematic biology. This parallel is the ever recurring need to delimit classes of organisms—genera, families, orders, even phyla—and of validating the criteria both of their delimitation and of their grouping, and of justifying the why and how of such judgments.

Civilizations resemble organic classes in being natural systems. That is, they can be said to possess both a structure and a content within this structure. By contrast one can hardly speak of the events of history as possessing a structure or filling a system. True, the structure and content of civilizations do change. And such changes of cultural structure are events—institutional events they might be called; and they are due to or expressed in straight-out historical events such as the Declaration of Independence, or the Fall of the Bastille, or Appomattox. This linkage is the reason, or one reason, why civilizations and their structured content, namely institutions and cultural patterns, enter into history. Civilizations in fact might be roughly defined as the residue of history when one abstracts the events in history.

In short, the problem of the definition and delimitation of civilizations is a generically and genuinely historical one even though the methods of conventional historiography as such hardly extend to its solution.

For instance, the historical principles of continuity or gradation and of unity of interconnection hold for civilizations much as they do for historic flows. It has by now become clear that some relations have existed between different cultures—all human cultures, high and low—as far back as we can trace them, even into the Palaeolithic. Reference is not to similarity of customs and institutions springing repeatedly and independently—spontaneously as it were—out of a common stock of human nature. Reference is rather to connections due to migrations, to contacts and transfers, to learning and exposure to new ideas. In short, these are connections of a specifically historical character, and in principle substantiable by historical evidence, even though the times are so remote, or the geographic ranges so great, that documentary evidence is broken or lacking—surviving at best in fragments. In such cases archaeological or other inferential, indirect evidence takes the place of documented and direct evidence. The meetings of men with men, or their ideas, and the results of such encounters, do remain historical events by whatever means they may be determined or verified. And the number of such inferred historical connections—counting only those conservatively substantiated—is now so great that the existence of a vast web of ancient and recent interrelations of peoples and their cultures, the world over, has become indubitable.

For instance, there is the alphabet, invented once only, on the western edge of Asia, but spread, by 1500, from Ireland and Morocco to Korea and Luzon, in a hundred styles and scripts, but all connected in origin and traceable derivation—and by 1951 extended over the globe.

There is knowledge of the metallurgy, manufacture, and use of iron, again originating once only—apparently not far in space and time from the invention of the alphabet—and diffusing equally far, and but little faster.

There is the ritual complex familiar to us from Romans, Greeks, and ancient West Asiatics in which animals were ceremonially dedicated and slaughtered at altars, their blood—or other select but usually inedible parts—given to the gods, and their flesh eaten by the worshipers; so that every important sacrifice was also a banquet, and a meat feast came to presuppose worship. With this complex there is usually associated the further practice of divining the future by inspection of the victims' entrails, especially their livers. Liver divination is known from Mesopotamia a millennium before Homer and the Etruscans. The simultaneous sacrifice of swine, sheep, and cattle—the suovetaurilia—is recorded contemporaneously from Rome and from Chou China. Blood sacrifice, sometimes with associated divination, has maintained itself until today in India, in Manchuria, in the Philippines and Borneo, in Negro Africa.

Until a generation ago, anthropologists tended to assume that this widespread occurrence meant that blood sacrifice and entrail divination were practices spontaneously flowing from human nature, from something immanent in the mind, which was likely to come to the surface almost anywhere and express itself in the institution of more or less parallel customs. Such a simple and placid assumption may no longer be made. The absence of this ritual complex from large areas of our planet, including all of native Australia, Polynesia, and America, forbids its explanation as due merely to a spontaneous generation out of ever present impulses in the constitution of man. In short, explanation in terms of inherent psychology is no longer possible; but the institution remains as a cultural phenomenon, as an invention or created device; and as such it must have a history—even if it no longer possesses a "necessary" origin.

As between one ramifying history or several coalescing histories for blood sacrifice, the first is indicated as more likely by the parallel cases of the alphabet and ironworking, to which can be added others such as money coinage, monasticism, chess. For each of these a unique history, though an intricate and branching one, has been documentarily traced without undue lacunae in the connecting evidence.

Human culture thus no longer is something that we believe we can derive directly from psychology, but it is construed as a historic product whose history can be gradually reconstructed and is being reconstructed. The cases just cited are inventions or institutions common to, but also restricted to, Asia, Europe, and nearer Africa. A smaller number of culture traits have gradually worked their way, beginning some tens of thousands of years ago, into the other continents and remoter lands and islands. Fire, techniques of stoneworking, the domesticated dog, the idea of spirit possession, transvestitism, the art of whaling, are examples. The differences between these fewer but more world-wide transmission growths and the first-cited Eurasian ones are in the infrequency of communications, lesser intensity of the influences, and increased lacunae in the evidence, rather than in principle.

For the great Old World main land mass within what the Greeks knew as the Oikoumenê, the traced and specific interconnections are now so many that a really separate total history of any culture in the area can no longer be thought of. China got from the West its wheat and its cattle, its bronze and its iron, presumably its divine kingship and retainer burial, its eunuchism, possibly the stimulus for its writing. It gave to the West silk, paper, and porcelain, playing cards, the idea of the dragon, probably gunpowder, perhaps alchemy and printing. How much of Chinese civilization was native Chinese in origin, and how much imported?—from ancient Mesopotamia, from Europe, from Persia and India—like Buddhism, for instance. How much of our Western civilization is the creation of ourselves and our blood ancestors, and how much of it has come to us from Rome and Greece, from Judaea and Phoenicia, from Mesopotamia and India and China? Most anthropologists and culture historians would agree that in probably every human society, the major part of the content of its culture or civilization has been derived from outside.

However, with such a finding once accepted as a principle, consequences ensue—at least for the comparative student whose subject is the development of human culture. The historian *de métier* will be less troubled. If he is telling the history of Europe, one of his tasks will be to trace the rise, the development, the effects of firearms in the West, and it does not too much affect his interpretation whether gunpowder was first compounded in China, in Western Asia, or by Berthold Schwartz. And conversely the historian of China can trace the spread of Buddhism in China, the rise of its sects, its obstacles and influence within the country, without having first to master the full story of the origin of the religion and its trials and accomplishments in India. But the comparative student does have to face such wider problems—not only if his subject matter is cultural items such as firearms or Buddhism whose course runs across societies and nations, but perhaps even more if his subject is integral cultures, civilizations as such in their continuities, superficially coterminous with their societies.

Yet if Chinese civilization is mostly not Chinese in source, it can not really be coterminous as a concept with Chinese society, in

DELIMITATION OF CIVILIZATIONS

any strict sense. And if this is so what makes it an entity that can be systematically compared with India and the West, with Egypt or Rome?

The historian as such cannot answer this problem because his frame of operation is normally cultural or intracultural, not transcultural. But he has his own version of the type of problem. Shall the delimitation between Ancient and Mediaeval-Modern history be set at 476? Or at 330, as was customary not so long ago? Or at "around 500"? Or perhaps at 622, as might seem definitely appropriate for western Asia and not too inappropriate for Europe? There is more involved here than a technical taxonomic boundary in the stream of continuous happenings. Ancient history is the story of the later phase, the Greek and Roman phase, of the old Mediterranean civilization. Mediaeval and Modern history on the other hand constitute the story of the development of Occidental Christian civilization, only partly overlapping with the Mediterranean in geography. A transcultural segregation of civilizational entities is thus implied, and touched on, in any setting of the boundary between the Ancient and the Mediaeval-Modern flow of events in the most elementary and conventional of historic classifications.

Let us examine the factors or considerations that enter into this or any similar delimitation.

Where it is only a question of simple narrative flow, a striking event of obvious significance suffices for practical purposes: the "fall" of Rome, or transfer of the capital to Constantinople. The historiographer points out that his boundary or starting point is a convenient symbol rather than a cataclysmic event that wiped out all antecedents. He may even point out that conditions were more alike immediately across the date boundary, say as between 475 and 477, than as between years on one side of it but spaced farther apart, such as 477 and 497. But, such cautions once observed, and a résumé given of the condition of affairs just before 476, the historiographer is no longer conscious of a problem, because his main course thereafter lies within the range of a single civilization. At most he may have to decide whether Byzantium and Russia were historically in Europe, or when Russia entered European civilization.

But when the frame of consideration is avowedly comparative and world wide, some attitude must be taken toward delimitation if inquiry is to attain to more results than the tracing of innumerable separate lines of crisscrossing interconnections. If there is any question of uniformities in history or recurrent regularities in civilization that can be empirically determined, the attack must be comparative. And valid comparison presupposes that the unit civilizations which are the matrix in which the regularities recur, be comparable entities; in short that they be definable.

Let us now review some of the criteria of delimitation.

1. *Discontinuity in Space or Time*.—When one civilization has ended before another has begun—such as Egyptian in relation to our own; or when they are situated far apart—China and Europe, for instance—their separateness is so obvious that the question of delimitation ordinarily does not rise to consciousness. The problem must obtrude when they are continuous, contiguous, or both. Greece-Rome and the West; Russia and Western Europe; Byzantium and Russia; China and Japan; Maya and Toltec-Aztec are cases. It is then that other criteria than space-time discontinuity are needed.

2. *Language*.—Separate civilizations regularly possess distinct languages. However, as a practical criterion this fact does not attain serious significance because speech tends to change with time and distance rapidly enough for repeated mutual unintelligibilities usually to arise within the area and the duration of a civilization—at least of a major civilization whose society is numbered by millions. This is not a theorem that speech changes faster than culture, which would be hard to vindicate because its terms would be hard to define. The fact is merely that when speech has diverged to a certain degree it is no longer intelligible, and its several forms have lost the faculty of interinfluence and assimilation which as dialects they still possessed.

Indeed, civilizations are more often than not bilingual or multilingual. Thus, Sumerian and Semitic in earlier Mesopotamia;

Aryan and Dravidian in India; Greek and Latin in balance in the Roman Empire; Western Europe with more than a dozen languages—and indeed, based on these, of late as many rampant and rival nationalisms. In fact, Danilevsky considered it an advantage for a civilization if it could grow up in a society of moderate speech diversity, languages diversified into distinctness but not to the point of their having lost sense of their underlying connectedness.

A decisive civilization evidently tends strongly to establish a sort of superlanguage throughout its confines—a language of power and culture, of court or literature. Mandarin, Sanskrit, the Greek Koinê, Latin in Western Christendom, Arabic in Islam, Great Russian in Soviet civilization—these are familiar examples. This metropolitan language is not an outrightly fabricated one, but normally is a local dialect that attains prestige association and becomes the standardized speech of government, class, and cultivation—of religion also, if that is standardized. A distinctive script tends strongly to be associated with this official and supernational language of the civilization, and reinforces it. Sometimes vernaculars pursue their courses of growth and differentiation beneath the supernational language and finally largely displace it, except in ritual; as in Europe and in India.

3. *Religion.*—An institutionalized and codified religion tends to accompany each empirical civilization unit: Catholicism, Orthodoxy, Islam, Brahmanism, in some measure Confucianism. These might be called world religions or universal religions as Latin, Greek, Arabic, Sanskrit, Mandarin are world languages—each universal in intent for its cultural world at the top level.

The early Near Eastern civilizations differed from the others in not producing such organized institutional religions. Worship remained an aggregation of local cults. Hence when the civilizations were long-lived, their associated fortuitous cult religions might crumble away before them, and in any event did not survive them. On the contrary, where religions came with an impulse toward institutionalization, toward absorption of other segments of the culture or association with the state, they survived the autonomy of their civilization and state. Mazdaism, Judaism, Christianity are examples. Mohammedanism went even farther and founded its civilization, religion, state, and universal language at one moment and as one interrelated whole.

Toynbee has developed the fact of the frequent association of a civilization with a religion into a general principle for explaining the transformations of culture, the development of one civilization out of another. The religion of an old civilization becomes the chrysalis or pupa, as it were, from which after a time it reëmerges clad in the body of a new civilization. Basically, this idea seems to rest on the origin of Christianity toward the end of the course of Helleno-Roman civilization, coupled with its dominance during the subsequent European civilization. Spengler already sensed the incongruity of this historic fact; and, cultures being for him monadal and incommensurable each had of necessity to possess its own distinctive religion. He therefore invented a Magian culture of which Christianity was the religious side. Toynbee's chrysalis view makes fewer assumptions, and receives partial confirmation from at least one other example. Indian Mahayana Buddhism, carried to China and established there between Han and T'ang, helped to differentiate Mediaeval China from Ancient China—into at least a new phase if not a wholly separate civilization.

However, other applications of Toynbee's chrysalis concept fit less happily. In the case of his Syro-Hebrew-Iranian civilization or "Syriac Society," its universal church is said to be Islam, but its universal state is first the Achaemenian empire, later its reintegration in the Abbasid caliphate—a thousand years of arrested pupation thus being at least partly transferred from religion to state. All this is in the general area and period for which Spengler felt compelled to invent his Magian-Arabic civilization. The ingenuities and assumptions of both writers are obviously due to the fact that the region and era are one in which several civilizations were in unusually complex interrelation, and their delimitation is therefore particularly difficult.

4. *Political and Military Development.*—An idea of some sort of rule, dominion, or preëminence of strength has long been

intertwined with that of civilization and remains associated with it. Indeed the first form taken by the concept of a series of civilizations was that of a succession of empires: Assyrian, Persian, Macedonian, Roman, Holy Roman. Toynbee still sees empire, the "universal state," as one of the final stages or factors in his formula of the normal course of civilizations. There is no doubt that a wide dominance quickly adds éclat, wealth, influence, and prestige and draws ability to itself. The center, at least, stabilizes, and internal development may result.

At the same time, correlation between degree of power and degree of creative civilization seems definitely low. There are too many cases of one without the other: Persians, Byzantines, Mongols, Turks on the one hand, Renaissance Italy and pre-Napoleonic Germany on the other. To be sure these are instances, strictly, of national rather than multinational dominance without cultural brilliance, or the reverse. But their geographical scope is mostly close to that of civilizations, and uni-national civilizations do occur. The one rule that appears to be without exception in this field is that no subject and exploited people or group of peoples has contributed significantly to a major burst of civilization. But this finding so conforms to common-sense expectation as hardly to need further comment.

5. *Economy and Technology.*—It is probable also that a great civilization can hardly arise without the presence of an economic surplus. This need perhaps not take the form of monetary capital; and it has perhaps most often gone primarily to a privileged segment of the population; but these considerations do not infringe the basic principle. It is also clear that in so-called primitive societies, the non-literate ones, there exists an obviously strong correlation between presence of a fairly steady economic reserve beyond subsistence needs on the one hand, and degree of organization of religion in ritual, belief, hierarchical structure, and aesthetic expression on the other. Now religious organization is not, in itself, the same as advancement in civilization; but it is obviously one of its indices.

The real difficulty with using the economy as a factor of civilization is a practical one: the difficulty of investigating it historically. Our age is statistical-minded about wealth. Most others were not, and they have left us haphazard opinions, wild guesses or wilder claims, or bits of incidental information so fragmentary as to add up only to extrapolated and uncertain totals. In subjectively rateable fields such as the course of philosophy, mathematics, literature, and sculpture, not to mention law and politics, we can establish advances and declines between, say, the Athens —or Greece—of 480 and that of 380 far more surely and accurately than we can for its economy or its wealth. Economics may be the more objective field, but for much of history its preserved data are much the more meager.

As for technology, the situation is rather different since new inventions do tend to leave their mark, especially in archaeology. If nevertheless the correlation of inventions with entities of high civilization is not conspicuously high, it is because technological advances tend both to be permanent acquisitions and to diffuse beyond the inventing nation, even to wholly alien civilizations, as we have seen. The invention of bronzeworking, of coinage, of seaworthy ships, of deep well drilling, of the riding of horses and again of riding with stirrups, of letters and then of printing —all these were probably originally either causes or signs or products of some local cultural florescence; but they soon became more than that, and ended as universal international property. Technological advances are the most persistently accumulative, and therefore ultimately the most intercivilizational, of all cultural innovations. Consequently they can be used for the delimitation of particular civilizations only with reserve and in special situations.

6. *Style.*—Probably the best indicators of civilizational delimitations, in our present stage of understanding, are the activities subject to the factor of style. These are the cultural activities that are most overtly "creative," most markedly qualitative, and also most transient on the whole. Here are to be included as a matter of course not only all the arts, but also intellectual creativities such as philosophy and science, and more frivolous ones like

DELIMITATION OF CIVILIZATIONS 15

fashion. Science must definitely be included on account of its "historical behavior." For while the results of science tend to be permanent and to become universal like those of technological creation, yet the productivity of science comes as definitely in bursts or spurts as originality and high quality occur in spurts in the arts.

Most civilizations seem fairly early to develop a set of characteristic basic styles to which they then adhere as long as they continue. This persistence is most evident in the visual arts whose products survive or are later retrieved by archaeology. Such a style, in three-dimensional and relief sculpture as well as in painting, and largely in architecture also, was formed in Egypt in the first and second dynasties and was maintained almost unaltered from the third to the thirty-first: it persisted for centuries after the nation had lost its independence. In Mesopotamia, while art remains are fewer and somewhat less consistent, the same holds. No one would ever confuse the statuary or the carvings or seals of Egypt and those of Mesopotamia; they are as distinct in their patterns of form as are the Hieroglyphic and Cuneiform scripts. In China the typical art forms and attitudes were essentially achieved under Han, and some go back to Chou and even Shang. Imageless Islam developed the Arabesque manner to a superlative pitch. Greek styles continued through the Roman period into Christian times.

Much the same holds in other aesthetic activities. In the ancient Near East, literature early attained to an effective prose as well as to the device of antithetical or balanced statement for formalized or impassioned utterance, but it achieved no verse of strict form of any kind. In contrast, China, India, and Greece composed poetry from the first. Whether this was organized on a basis of syllable, quantity, stress, tone, rhyme, or strophe depended partly on the qualities of the languages; but once the instruments of form had been selected, they were retained throughout the course of the civilization. Also, the Chinese manner consistently cultivated brevity as well as sobriety; the Indian, length, exuberance, and exaggeration; the Greek, variety of compass and range of tone and intensity. When, a thousand years later, Islamic civilization suddenly formed, it started with certain Arabic meters, nuances, and themes, and has retained these, and imparted them to its Persian and Turkish derivatives, with only minor modifications and additions.

Even in matters like dress, similar idiosyncrasies and persistences of civilization are often manifest. In China, the Occident, Greece, Islam—in each not only was the type or basic cut of clothing characteristic, but so was its distinctive aim or ideal, the focus around which fashion spun.

Histories of art accordingly promise to be of increasing importance in the comparative history of civilizations. Art expresses values. It deals with them perhaps more directly than any other cultural activity. And in every civilization there resides, as one of its fundamentals, a value system. This value system is ramified, only partly explicit, sometimes not wholly consistent, subject to development—but in one sense it also is what holds the civilization together and comes nearest to summating it. That the arts should be one of the main expressions of this value system and perhaps its most sensitive index, is no wonder. Only, the arts must be construed in their widest sense, from the arts of conduct and manners, even of cooking, to those of the intellect in science, philosophy, and religious speculation.

Systems of value are elusive to fix, difficult to describe. They find, however, an objective expression in their histories, which record the first development of potentialities, their growth, their realization with saturation of the patterns achieved, the consequent repetitious atrophy or, alternatively, rupture of pattern. These histories are the documented records leading to culminations or florescences—in the arts, sciences, philosophy, sometimes accompanied by bursts of achievement also in government, wealth, and general prosperity. The peaks of the growth profiles in the several activities may come closely clustered in time, as in Greece and Islam, or more widely spaced as in China, India, and the West; or repetitively as in Egypt. They are however historically determinable phenomena, not subject to material dispute

DELIMITATION OF CIVILIZATIONS 17

as regards their actuality. The courses of such culminations are perhaps as close to constituting reasonable uniformities as occur in history. This intercultural uniformity is not primarily in content but in the form taken by the historic process; not in events, but in the pattern of events as something tending to recur; and it is connected in its occurrence with those distinctive larger aggregations or nexuses of culture which we call civilizations.

To summarize. To the historian, civilizations are large, somewhat vague segments of the totality of historical events which it may sometimes be convenient or useful to segregate off from the remainder of history, and which tend to evince certain dubiously definable qualities when so segregated. To the student of culture, civilizations are segments of the totality of human history when this is viewed less for its events, and less as behavior and acts, than as the more enduring products, forms, and influences of the actions of human societies. To the student of culture, civilizations are segregated or delimited from one another by no single criterion: partly by geography, partly by period; partly by speech, religion, government, less by technology; most of all, by those activities of civilization that are especially concerned with values and the manifest qualities of style. This is an area of subject matter peripheral to the historian, but increasingly in his view. Culture is most easily conceived as a static generalization of collective behavior suppressing event in favor of nontransitory form. Yet it is increasingly evident that no civilization is ever actually static. It always flows. Like style, it is qualitative, structured form in process. The form and structure possessed by civilizations invite a comparative morphology. Yet that the forms are always in process means that they are also historic phenomena and must be viewed historically. The point at which historical examination and morphological inquiry seem most fruitfully to intersect is in the phenomenon of culmination which civilizations share with styles.

2. Have Civilizations a Life History?

HAVE CIVILIZATIONS a life history? And in what sense have they a life history?

Some might be tempted to ask, first, in what degree civilizations are really separate, are genuinely distinguishable one from the other. Logically the query is fair, since history is continuous and since some kind of degree of what the anthropologist calls culture is possessed by every society. However, our basic question really also implies a partial answer. When we speak of civilizations, as we must when we want to compare them, it is axiomatic that they are plural and therefore separate—separate enough to distinguish. What our question accordingly comes to is, first of all, how far are we justified to go in separating or distinguishing civilizations; and next, how far are these separate civilizations nevertheless repetitive, recurrent, and similar in type and in their individual histories.

The first part of this revised question, as to separateness, need only be met with common opinion based on common knowledge of the difference of civilizations. There is no doubt as to our contemporary Western civilization, that of China, and that of ancient Egypt being distinct. True, we share wheat and barley with the old Egyptians and with the Chinese; and cattle and pigs; and use of bricks and masonry, and iron and copper—knowledges

---

Reprinted by permission from *Centennial*, American Association for the Advancement of Science, Washington, D. C., September, 1948, pp. 9-13. [Collected papers presented at the Centennial Celebration.]

that have been handed down from one generation to another and spread from one country to another. There is always some sharing by civilizations of their content. But there are also the things that are specific, particular, not shared; traits that are distinctive. Such is our writing not with hieroglyphs—nor with ideographic characters—but with letters of the Roman alphabet. Or again, our being Christians, instead of Buddhists or worshipers of animal-headed gods. Or living amidst our contemporary surroundings and equipments of steel, instead of stone plus a little bronze and less iron. Nor do we of Western civilization try to mummify our dead; nor recite magic spells; nor obey kings whom we equate with the sun god or with heaven; and so on.

Our problem really begins once the difference and separateness of civilizations are granted, when we go on to inquire what recurring likeness there is that links the several civilizations as exemplars of a type. What have they in common that we may justly consider them all as cases of one kind—all as individuals of one species?

It is evident that most major civilizations are supernational. Each is ordinarily shared, not quite identically but essentially, by a number of nations politically independent, distinctive in language, and possessed each of a sense of constituting a well-marked-off society. Thus, Western or Occidental civilization is shared by Americans, Latin Americans, Canadians, French, British, Germans, Italians, and other European nations. Each of these peoples possesses a slightly different national version of the common Western civilization; the differences are obviously minor. All these nations are Christian, all write with the Roman alphabet, all elect parliamentary representatives who alone can levy taxes, and so on. Again, the Islamic or Mohammedan civilization comprises Arabs, Berbers, Persians, Turks, Indians, and Malays. The Far Eastern civilization includes Chinese and Japanese, and also Koreans and Annamese—all in separate countries as well as separate ethnic groups. The ancient Classical civilization was Greek and Roman—double-barreled even in name—with many submerged nationalities included. Egyptian civilization, at its long range from us, looks superficially uninational, but it was formed when the peoples of lower and upper Egypt united, and it came to include Lybians and Nubians.

A first-rank or major civilization thus is normally multinational and multilingual, though it may possess one standard language of higher culture. It is spontaneously participated in by a whole series of peoples, who are usually at the same time proud and jealous of their governmental independence. They may frequently fight among themselves. Yet they share much the greater part of their civilization, and all the essentials. A civilization thus is something that has grown up of itself into a supernational product—has achieved without trying a scale of unity and integration which Leagues of Nations and United Nations are still struggling precariously to attain in the political field.

As Toynbee says, a civilization can be defined as the unit of historical intelligibility—the minimum unit that makes entire sense in history. The history of England is not fully intelligible in itself, that of France is not intelligible, that of Germany and Italy are not. All are too much basically alike in their culture and ideologies, therefore too interrelated, too influenced by one another, for the isolated history of any one of these countries to be explainable wholly in terms of itself.

Toynbee goes on to recognize "universal empire," embracing the entire area of the culture, unfortunately usually by conquest, as one of the normal or expectable later stages of a civilization. Spengler holds the same idea—he makes great empire the final phase of civilization. Cultural internationalism thus normally precedes political internationalism. Furthermore, civilizations not only are big things, but they grow larger early in their careers, earlier than big states or empires; and they grow large automatically, by spread or persuasion or attraction, rather than by force.

Let us now consider what the several great civilizations have in common besides multinationalism. Presumably, they share their common features because common mechanisms are operative in their growth and existence and produce analogous results.

In this matter, we must distinguish between the thousands of cultural traits and elements that tend always to spread, and largely do spread, between civilizations by intercultural diffusion, and that which is specific to a particular civilization and characteristic of it alone. Most useful inventions obviously are of the first or diffusing class: railroads, the telegraph, radio—also parliamentary institutions. Somewhat earlier, printing, firearms, the mariner's compass, clocks and watches, windmills spread. Still earlier were the alphabet, millstones and waterwheels, also ironworking and steel tempering, and coined money. Back beyond all of these in the dimmer past were metallurgy, agriculture, blood sacrifice, and divination by omens. Innovations manage to spread faster today; but they did spread also in ancient and even in primitive times. These elements of civilization diffuse not only internationally but interculturally, from one civilization to another, as we have seen. We may call them the bricks of which each civilization builds its own distinctive edifice, distinctive because it follows its own plan or design. It is this over-all design which most characterizes a civilization and individuates it into something unique.

We might designate this over-all design of each civilization its fundamental ideology, its master plan. Oswald Spengler, prophet of doom, highly intuitive but also highly dogmatic, called it the "soul" of each culture, and believed these "souls" to be impermeable monads which could not really influence each other. Arnold Toynbee, with a more plastic interpretation, and with inclination toward morality rather than toward blind fate, sees the basic ideology as something akin to religion. He designates it, in fact, as the universal church or religion, universal within its own civilization, or aiming to be so. And he has worked out how it comes to be, and what the effect is. As a civilization grows old, he says, there is a tendency for its ruling class, its dominating minority, more and more to exploit the whole society. The exploited majority, the proletariat, seeks refuge or solace in a new cult or religion—like Christianity in the late Roman Empire times, or Mahayana Buddhism in the Chinese Empire of the same period. Finally the civilization perishes, as the society is rent to pieces by struggles between its minority and majority and is finished perhaps by an "external proletariat" of hitherto excluded barbarian hordes. But the evolved religion stands firm: it becomes a sort of chrysalis or pupa within which the old society and civilization transform into a new one. This new civilization therefore has the religion as its basic ideology, not only for dogma, but also as regards ethics, law, ideals, and custom. Thus Christianity served as the chrysalis by which the old, dying Graeco-Roman civilization was transformed into our Western or Occidental one: Christianity may be considered the core of our basic ideology, our cultural master pattern.

This mechanism does not hold in all cases, but it obviously does hold in some; and it is perhaps the most fruitful idea evolved by Toynbee, though recently he seems to have wavered regarding it. However, whether partly true or wholly true, the concept serves well to illustrate what is meant by the basic form, the fundamental design, the over-all plan of a civilization, as contrasted with its content of particular inventions, devices, fashions, manners, and other cultural items or elements. The concept also serves to show why civilizations tend to be large and supernational: these master plans are large things.

What such a master plan really is, other than a formal religion, is an assemblage of forms, a coördination of patterns. Now just what is meant by the term "cultural pattern"? A culture pattern means: a style of art; or a way of thinking; a philosophical point of view or attitude of faith; a set of manual habits and technological skills; or rules for getting on satisfactorily with one's fellow men. Taken all together, these styles, ways, attitudes, and rules add up to a more or less coherent design for a society's living. Living in the natural world is part of the design, as well as living with other humans. Also included is living with a reasonable degree of consistency, order, and dependability: for people want to live in harmony with themselves, instead of incessantly starting out on randomly different and unpredictable courses. Hence the master-plan design tends to be consistent. Even though a given society begins with a haphazard, ill-assorted culture, its normal drift will be toward greater coördination. Spengler sensed the coördination but exaggerated it into a mystic completeness. Tempering the Spengler concept down from its absoluteness, we see the coördination as something tangible, natural, and having survival value.

At any rate, every civilization must be accepted as more than the sum of its component items—as a wall is more than a thousand bricks. And evidently the most important thing to know about any civilization is what this "more than" is—what is its principle of coördination, its more or less successfully unifying plan.

We can then construe a civilization as something that achieves a degree of unity, that works from a start of more or less randomness toward increasing coherence, and that moves from amorphousness toward definiteness, from fumbling trials to decision. Any civilization will tend to move in this direction on the way toward its culmination; and its peak or apogee can be considered to be the point beyond which the master plan no longer shows increase in plastic coördination, but begins to fall apart, or to harden into rigidity, or both.

What is true for the whole of a civilization is likely to be perhaps even more true for its parts, whether these be economic, intellectual, political, artistic, or religious. Each of these parts of a civilization, unless interfered with by outside civilizations or by catastrophes of nature, usually shows during the ascendant phase of its history a growth toward definiteness, toward smoothness of control and achievement. The patterns of each become more firm of outline, more apt and consistent, more solid in content: they realize increasingly better what they aim at. One activity or art may have the start on another, such as sculpture over painting; or it may mature more rapidly, or keep developing longer. Thus the several activities usually do not synchronize exactly and may have their peaks string along for some centuries. But as parts of the same civilization, they are expectably at least roughly contemporary or overlapping, as well as interconnected.

This process of cultural growth from shadowy, groping beginnings, through selective commitment, to particular forms or patterns and growing control of these until they are achieved and their potentialities are realized—this process seems to be basic in the history of civilization. Its operations constitute what we call the rise of civilizations; its cessation or reversal, their decline or disintegration. The process is perhaps most readily distinguished in the arts and sciences: possibly because these move more nearly in orbits of pure pattern, relatively detached from the disturbances of natural accidents and social oppressions, conflicts and catastrophes. But in principle, the process would seem to be operative in all domains or segments of civilization.

Like every idea, this one may not be applied simplistically and mechanically. Not every civilization has a history of simple rise and fall. Room must be left for complications of structure and development. A society may seem to attain a realization of the patterns which it gradually evolved and shaped; but then, instead of either stereotyping or smashing these patterns and therewith dissolving its civilization, it may pause, take stock, look around, and make a fresh start with reconstituted patterns—wider or deeper or fuller patterns—at any rate, partly new ones. We have in such a case a renewed pulse of activity within the same culture. Thus in Europe the High Mediaeval and intensively Christian Gothic architecture and Gothic sculpture and contemporary literature had mainly achieved their aims, had realized themselves, around 1300. But Western civilization did not therewith enter upon fossilization or disintegration. Instead, it appeared to halt, to feel about, prospect, explore, for a century or so; and then it began to move onward again with reconstituted and more ambitious patterns, increasingly secular patterns, as the Renaissance pulse or phase. This Renaissance phase included successful painting, science exploration, and music which had been but insignificantly developed in the earlier Mediaeval phase.

Later again, that very Renaissance science which had flashed out so brightly with Copernicus appeared to reach a dead end after Newton. It faltered, paused for forty or fifty years, but then got itself moving again, around 1750, in new ways and in new directions. It used far more experimentation than before, and for the first time it grappled seriously and effectively with problems of chemistry, geology, and biology. True, there is only one basic stream of Western science since Copernicus; but it is also true that this science comes in two tides or pulses—marked by a withdrawal and return, in Toynbeean phrase.

Such a hesitant pausing and reconstitution may involve the whole of a civilization, all of its activities, as it did in China around A.D. 200, with irruption of barbarians and gradual acceptance of a new universal church by the mass of the common people. Toynbee accordingly recognizes not "the" Chinese civilization as it is treated in conventional history as a single perduring unit, but two Chinese civilizations, a mother and a daughter civilization, within one and the same area. China I and China II we might call them—or, as he names them, the Sinic and the Main Body Far Eastern.

Spengler, always impatient and doctrinaire, also sees a break around A.D. 200. But he recognizes only China I; China II existed, he admits, as a series of events and some billions of lives, but without significance as a civilization: it possessed no master pattern or "soul," it created nothing. These two interpretations by Toynbee and Spengler certainly clash. The fact is, we have not yet known Chinese history very long nor do we understand it deeply, and there is still room for much difference of judgment, even though there be approximate agreement as to the criteria which constitute a civilizational growth. At any rate, this extreme case serves as warning that the problems we are dealing with cannot be solved too offhandedly by any simple witching-rod of a yardstick.

A corollary of the foregoing findings concerns genius. Great men notoriously cluster in time and place: in Periclean Athens, in Augustan Rome, in the Italian Renaissance, in Elizabethan England. There they shine like thickly set constellations; outside, are long periods of great voids. The pattern and master-pattern interpretation of civilization explains this clustering. Great men can appear only while great patterns are in the shaping during the life history of a civilization. At other times native genius is wasted —it has nothing to take hold of, it leaves no achievement that permanently means something. But in the culminating cultural pattern, the genius realizes himself.

There is really strong evidence to support this view. Biologically, by all we know of the normal workings of heredity, geniuses and talents should be born at a fairly steady rate, the same as morons and idiots. They ought to appear averaging about the same in number per million of population. But they do not so appear in history: they notoriously come in crowded bursts, and then there are long near-vacancies. The discrepancy must be due to some nonbiological factor which checks or neutralizes biology. What can this factor be but civilization? Especially when we see how each civilization normally has its successive phases of dimness, of gathering, of full unfolding, then of slowing up, of dying away; and that the overwhelming majority of the men whom we unanimously recognize as great have lived in the great periods of great civilizations.

There is an inescapable correlation between genius and phase of civilization. Without great men being born, it is true, the finest and most valuable products of civilization would of course not get produced. But without civilizations, there would be no great men. They would exist potentially, but they would not be actualized: they would find no opportunity, no expression.

Genius then is a function of stage or phase of pattern development in civilizations. It serves as an index of cultural development. The genius, considered as an individual, contains a psychological component and problem—though a very complex problem. Considered socioculturally, genius can be seen as product and as indicator of his civilization. And the civilization of which he serves as index is not something fixed and static, but is in its very nature flowing and developmental.

This functional dependence of actualized genius on culture pattern is something that Toynbee does not deal with and Spengler only adumbrates.

When we review all the times and lands on earth that have contained human beings possessing some measure of culture, it quickly becomes clear that a great majority of the generations have fallen into primitive times, or into featureless, low-patterned and low-profiled civilizations, or into the groping and unformed phases of civilizations which did culminate or into their decadent or already fossilized ones. The proportion of negative generations, those unable to produce genius, has amounted surely to four-fifths of the total, and may have been nine-tenths or more.

It looks like a heavy indictment of culture that it should prevent realization of 90 per cent of the geniuses to whom biological heredity gave the requisite endowment. It is an indictment: at any rate it is such until we become aware that the 10 per cent of achieved geniuses are also the product of civilization—unconditionally so. With no kind or degree of civilization, actualized genius would be 100 per cent suppressed.

Incidentally, so far as high performance and genius are largely a function of phase of civilization, the already generally discredited theory of racism or innate race superiorities obviously has another prop knocked out from under it.

The proposition as to the basic importance of stage of civilization may sound categorical. It has been put baldly and bluntly, because to me it appears unequivocally true; and it also seems important. Even more to the point, however, is another finding: namely, that definite answers to problems of magnitude can be extracted from the history of civilizations when the data are examined by genuine sociocultural methods, that is, with reference to process. Sociocultural process means the relation of pattern to pattern within successive developmental stages of civilizations, these civilizations themselves being viewed each as a total unit and ultimately also in comparison with one another. Resulting answers are not simple and they are not easy; but it begins to appear that they are being attained.

3. The Time Profile of Western Civilization

OUR OWN CIVILIZATION, the Western, grew up largely on the European part of the soil previously occupied by the Roman half of the Hellenic or Graeco-Roman or Classical civilization, but with some extensions beyond the former Roman frontier, as in Germany. The time of its beginning may be set somewhere between 500 and 900.

Toynbee says before 700. One might shade this more narrowly to 650, as the date perhaps marking most closely the nadir of barbarization intervening between the past Classical and the coming Western civilization. Spengler says 900, or sometimes tenth century, in referring to the birth of the Western culture; but with a gestation or "prodromal" period since 500.

In favor of the recognition of such an embryonic stage there are the following facts. By 500 all the Roman West was in barbarian power and political control, and the old Classical culture was in clear disintegration there; but nothing was yet apparent that was qualitatively suggestive of the future European civilization. However, around 900 or soon after, as Spengler observes, the main modern nationalities of Western Europe emerged: that is, they attained consciousness of themselves as nationalities. The first historical appearance of the French and German languages, as distinct from Latin and from Germanic vernaculars,

---

Reprinted by permission of the Wenner-Gren Foundation for Anthropological Research, Inc., New York City, from A. L. Kroeber, *A Roster of Civilizations and Culture*, Viking Fund Publications in Anthropology, No. 33 (1962), 87–96.

is in a tenth-century record of the Strasbourg oaths which the grandsons of Charlemagne gave each other in 842. Spengler's prodromal phase of 500–900 has the merit of doing something, conceptually, with Charlemagne's empire and the so-called Carolingian cultural renaissance. This Carolingian renaissance obviously underlay all Western civilization chronologically; and yet it left so little impress on this civilization as to be puzzling. If it was a revival, how could it have so little permanent effect? Was it therefore perhaps an abortive endeavor rather than an actual revival? In fact, in the century after Charlemagne, everything Carolingian disintegrated—the empire with its internationalism as well as much of the meager little rebirth of culture. The weakness accompanying the Carolingian disintegration is pregnantly illustrated by the fact that the peak period of Viking raiding and spoliation of the continent fell between 830 and 900. By contrast, the basic alignments that emerged during the following tenth century—whether national, social, or cultural alignments—have persisted until today under all the enrichments and modifications that have been added to them.

It has always been a question of what the Carolingian Empire and unification of Western Christian Europe—and this was the only political unification that Europe ever attained!—what Charlemagne's empire really meant, on long-range view. Apparently its significance lay in its declaration of autonomy. Charles the Great's empire declared the westerly Graeco-Roman civilization definitely dead, and the West now independent of the Byzantine survival of easterly Graeco-Roman civilization. Hence the suddenly overt tensions between West and East within the Christian Church at this period. The tensions and rift are instanced by the Pope's crowning of Charlemagne as Caesar in 800; by Charlemagne's intervention in the *filioque* doctrinal dispute in 809; by the council of Constantinople (869–870), and the quarrel of Photius with the Popes (Nicholas I and Leo VI); and by the contest of the Eastern and Western churches for the adhesion of Bulgaria. But the West was still too poor in material wealth and in cultural content to develop a real civilization under Charlemagne. So it had to begin over again, and much less pretentiously, a century or more later, when the Carolingian Empire had not only fallen to pieces but had been definitely superseded by the emerged nationalistic consciousness.

Western civilization has throughout remained multinational, "polyphonic and orchestral," as it then began in the 900's. It is of very real significance that Charlemagne's unification has never yet been successfully imitated in Europe, though Spaniards, French and Germans—reference is to Hitler, not to the mediaeval Holy Roman Empire, which was always an unrealized dream nostalgic for a form—successively have tried; and Russians are apparently now trying. Precedent is therefore against the Russians, if they belong to the Western civilization. Whereas if they represent an essentially separate civilization, as Danilevsky contended, there is no precedent for or against their prospects. In that case, the "youth" of Russian culture may mean either that it possesses greater vigor and strength than the older Western civilization, or that it is characterized by greater immaturity and fumbling.

The basic multinationalism of Western civilization is also evident from the fact that it had hardly begun to crystallize out when, within a generation of the year 1000, there were added to the French and German consciousnesses a further series of emerging nationalities: Polish, Hungarian, Scandinavian, English, which have persisted. Russia also attained its first national organization around 1000, but is not included here because this early state still lay wholly outside the Roman Catholic and Western sphere of influence. Decision would have to be made as between Canute the Dane, 1014–1035, or Alfred (848–899), with the latter construed as preceding 1000 because of English geographical nearness to the Franklish-North French center. There is a brief tabular collocation in my *Configurations of Culture Growth*, p. 726.

We may therefore conclude that at some time between 500 and 650 or 700 the essential detachment of Western Europe from Graeco-Roman civilization became effective; that from 650–700 on this autonomy began to come into the consciousness of Western societies and that these tended to assume first political cohesion and then national scope; and that around 900 or 950 the framework of the new culture began to fill, however humbly at first, with cultural content of its own creation. By 1100, with the Crusades, the youthful Western society had already become aggressive against the societies of the Byzantine and Arab Islamic civilizations—impracticably aggressive as regards permanent expansion, it is true, but nevertheless actually successful for a time.

This Western civilization is at the moment the dominant one in the world. Its ending has been repeatedly forecast: as follows. By Danilevsky, it was forecast to happen soon, whenever Russia shall become consolidated; because the West is already overripe. By Spengler, the prediction is for about 2200, Caesarism and the "civilization" phase having been entered on around 1800. By Toynbee, the end threatens and is indicated by numerous warning symptoms. This end may possibly happen soon, but it is by no means inevitable, because ultimate resources are moral and religious, and are therefore beyond real predictability. For my part, I refrain from long-range prophecy. It is tempting but usually unprofitable, practically as well as intellectually: its emotional repercussions tend to be high, its probability values low.

The course of this Western civilization of ours is remarkable for the strong degree of difference of content between its two main phases, which are usually called the Mediaeval and the Modern. The first, which culminated in the 1200's and really ended soon after 1300, is characterized by the power and success of the Church. It was in the High Mediaevalism of the West that Christianity reached the crowning success of its career. Christianity at that time achieved an organization and domination of society that were not only extraordinarily effective but were culturally productive and concordant. Mediaeval philosophy, architecture, and art are thoroughly religious and at the same time embody secular values of a high order. Other branches of Christianity—Greek, Slavic, Nestorian—were equally sincere and fervid, but they failed to produce even rudiments of anything comparable either aesthetically or intellectually.

Around 1300 and the ensuing decades the tight High Mediaeval Christian frame began to be unable to contain any longer the cultural creativity that was swelling within it. The earlier satisfaction afforded by mere existence within this frame, the essential indifference or hostility to everything outside it, now commenced to disappear. Knowledge of what lay beyond, knowledge of the past, secular knowledge became more and more sought. Religious feeling weakened, at least relatively. The Church as an organization fell into troubles: there happened the attempt of Anagni, the Popes at Avignon, the Great Papal Schism, the Hussite Revolt, the Councils that failed to result in reforms. Systematic scholastic philosophy virtually died as knowledge increased by leaps and bounds—knowledge of the world as well as inventions and technologies: gunpowder, printing, oil painting, seaworthy ships, spectacles, clocks, playing cards, Arabic numerals and algebra, casting of iron and other metallurgical processes. Not one of these had anything to do with religion or furthered religion, but they all enriched the civilization and the life under it. The Gothic arts continued for a time, on momentum. But they showed definite symptoms of decadence: flamboyancy, perpendicularity; or they were applied secularly to guild halls and tomb monuments, not to cathedrals. The Mediaeval profane vernacular literatures, lyrical and narrative, now became arid, allegorizing, or extravagant. Even the political structure shook. The monarchies receded from such mild strength as they had attained in the thirteenth century. Towns grew in wealth and strength but also in embroilments; feudalism was losing its hold, but no substitute for it had forged into consciousness. Politically, the two centuries were centrifugal and disruptive; in Spain and Germany as in France and England royal power receded.

Only northern Italy now marched forward to an affirmation and realization of cultural achievements; while in France, the Low Countries, Germany, and more or less in all the rest of Europe, culture, though growing, was at the same time floundering and sliding as a result of the progressive weakening of the traditional Mediaeval patterns. This was the period of the north Italian city-states; of growth of commerce and industry, as well as of applied science—spectacles, chimneys, "Arabic" arithmetic and calculation. It was also the time of great Italian literature, painting, architecture, sculpture, then of the foundation of great Italian music—in short, the Renaissance. The beginnings are around 1300, with Dante and Giotto as the symbols—both still Mediaeval in their thinking and feeling, but also initiators of a long line of illustrious personalities whose surge did not begin to enter full culmination until 1500 and was two centuries more in subsiding. This stretch of Italian greatness was achieved wholly without national political unity or military triumphs. It was briefer and more localized than the Mediaeval phase, and thus is perhaps more usefully construed as an interphase transition than as a phase in its own right.

Around 1550 or 1600—perhaps 1575 will serve fairly as a precise definition, though nothing of this sort occurs without gradation—the second main movement in the European symphony began to be played when the other west European countries drew abreast of Italy in wealth, refinement of manners, the arts, and the sciences, after having politically consolidated themselves into organized nation-states. This consolidation gave them a massive weight which before long put them culturally ahead, as regards productivity, of the free but fragmented Italian cities, or of the "duchies" into which most of these had been transformed or absorbed. Portugal, Spain, Holland, England, France successively achieved this new phase of activity. Meanwhile, with the Reformation, a degree of ideological and emotional autonomy from Italian supremacy was also attained by the northerly nations. This autonomy aided the northern nations, such as Germany, that remained nationalistically or culturally backward, to lay a foundation for greater accomplishment in a subsequent century.

Still later, after about 1750, industrialism, enormously rapid accumulation of wealth, experimental science, democracy, and liberalism developed especially in the northwesterly countries, and gave this corner of the continent an increasing precedence of strength, prestige, and influence, in which America came to share and, quite recently, to predominate. Now, this shift is fully familiar; also, like everything that touches us immediately, it is difficult to appraise in historical perspective. A complete understanding of this shift, if it could be attained, would no doubt be full of implications as to the future of our Western civilization—as to its "fate." But that is just what we are not considering at this moment when we are trying to define the *known* boundaries and organization of our civilization, not to guess or argue its future.

The upshot of our review, then, is this. Western civilization has throughout been multinational and Christian. After a gestatory period of some centuries, it entered a first full phase of about four hundred years in which all higher achievements were meshed into religion. This was the time of culmination of not only the church as an ecclesiastical institution but of Christianity as an ideology and affective nexus. There followed a two- or two-and-a-half century period of transition in which many or most of the patterns of this first phase were increasingly loosened and softened, while a set of modified or new patterns gradually formed which were to characterize the subsequent second or Modern phase. Creative cultural leadership in both phases was Transalpine, most centering in or near France; in the intervening transition time the leadership and influence were strikingly Cisalpine, except for a definite trickle down the Rhine into the Low Countries.

Italy as a segment of Western civilization thus culminated while the remainder of the West was formally uncreative through being in metamorphosis. But, as the northern and western countries got their second-phase patterns organized, by about 1575, Italy receded in innovation and influence. Italy's peculiar role within the civilization seems bound up first with its having been the political and prestige center of the last phase of the preceding Graeco-Roman civilization, with consequent tendency to retain remnants or remembrances of that civilization. Second, Italian particularity seems connected with having, perhaps on account of its retentions, resisted with a measure of success full acceptance of the High Mediaeval patterns with their barbarian

Transalpine provenience and "Gothic" feudal and non-Classical quality. And third, as these patterns were nevertheless at last partly accepted in Italy, but, by a sophisticated population which had never wholly left its towns, they blended with the vestiges and occasional recoveries of the former civilization on the same soil, and above all with the now unleashed creative energies of the people, and put Italy transiently into the van of Western civilization. This incidental or secondary element of rediscovery or revivification is what has given the Italian cultural surge the name of Renaissance. It was of course far more a birth than a rebirth; but there is some minor ingredient of the latter, as there is of persistence from Graeco-Roman civilization. At about the time when the impulses of this spurt were waning, the Transalpine peoples had begun to formulate their new pattern such as a dissenting cast of anticlerical Christianity, geographical discovery and expansion, centralized monarchy of power, noticeable accumulation of wealth. Blending with these what they took over from High Renaissance Italy in patterns of manners and art—as Italy had previously accepted some of their Mediaevalism—these northern and western nations attained to the full second phase of Western civilization. This phase in turn, from about 1750-1800 on, spread toward the margins of Europe—Germany, Scandinavia, the Slavic areas—and into the Americas.

If this characterization of the salient physiognomy of Western culture history is essentially correct, it has certain implications of a general and theoretical nature. Such general implications may be more important than even successful close-up predictions would be. The implications may in fact be what in the end will contribute most to our capacity to predict reliably. What this formulation shows is that the course of a large multinational civilization may be more complex than a smooth rise-culmination-and-decline; that it may come in successive surges or pulses—what we have called phases. It is further plain, so far as the preceding formulation is sound, that the intervals between the pulses may be, at least over most of the area of the civilization, periods of pattern dissolution, preparatory to pattern reconstruction.

Consequently, even if the mid-twentieth century is suffering from a breakdown of its cultural patterns—as is so often alleged and perhaps with most force and reason as regards the arts—the question still remains open whether such a breakdown is part of the final death of our civilization, as is sometimes feared or asserted; or on the contrary is merely symptomatic of an interpulse reconstruction. In the former case, Spengler's prophecies and Toynbee's fears would be right; in the latter, the present time would be only a sort of counterpart of what Transalpine Europe—most of Europe—was undergoing during the Italian Renaissance.

This question cannot be answered off-handedly in the context of the moment; and even less properly ought a too sure answer be given it at any time. The points to be summarized at this stage of our argument are essentially these. First, it is clear that civilizations are not simple, natural units that are easy to distinguish, or that segregate themselves out from the continuum of history on mere inspection. Second, the duration limits of any one civilization, the points of its beginning and ending, may also be far from easy to define. Instead of being something one begins with as evident, determination of the limits may be a problem in itself. If Toynbee can recognize China I and II and India I and II, why can we not recognize Western I and II?—with perhaps a Western III about to follow? Especially so since it is customary to accept without qualms Egypt *a, b, c, d*, even though not quite separate Egypts I, II, III, and IV. For all that has yet been shown one way or the other, the future may have in store not only Western III but perhaps even IV. In that event, our troubles of today would prove, when the full record shall be in, to be the reconstructive or the growing pains of the transition between phase II that ended say with the nineteenth century and a phase III that will perhaps reach its full beginning in the twenty-first.

Offhand, indeed, Western I and Western II—Mediaeval and Modern Europe—would seem probably to differ more in their patterns than China I from China II. That is, T'ang-Ming China would appear a less altered continuation of Shang-Han China, in spite of its addition of the new religion of Buddhism, than

Modern Europe is a continuation of Mediaeval Europe even though Christianity was maintained through both. To be sure, what is foreign and remote always seems more uniform and more continuous than the familiar. Accordingly a careful judicial weighing after intimate acquaintance with both sets of civilizations—if anyone possesses an equally sensitive acquaintance— might conceivably reverse the impression and leave us with the finding that Europe did indeed constitute a single though double-phase civilization, but that China was better construed as two successive civilizations, as Toynbee has it. Yet who could today press with honest assurance for the greater historic truth of either of the two alternatives? The problem is one of estimating the relative degree of difference between complex value-systems. For those interested in such judgments, it is intellectually fair and profitable to form impressions and opinions, but not to assert them beyond tentativeness. All we can really do at present is to ask ourselves questions of this kind, perhaps adding hesitant suggestions of answers. When a number of equipped minds shall have weighed the relevant evidence for perhaps some decades, their findings will carry real weight.

But, as long as we are essentially only asking, we can even now push our questioning farther. If we grant Toynbee's China I and II, and India I and II, and Mesopotamia I and II; and if we are ready to concede at any rate the possibility that the unity of Western civilization may properly be dissolved into Europe I and II; then why should not the taken-for-granted unit which Toynbee calls "Hellenic" civilization and Spengler "Classical" —why should not this be broken into its Greek and Roman components—in parallel terminology, Graeco-Roman I and II? Spengler simplifies the situation by recognizing only the "I" of China, India, and Mesopotamia, approximately, and refusing to discuss the "II's" as being merely frozen "civilizations," fellaheen petrifactions without living culture. But of course this is equivalent to recognizing the "II's." It is not their existence that Spengler denies—only their reaching a certain threshold of cultural worth.

For that matter, genuine consideration could be given this taxonomy:

Aegean	= Northeast Mediterranean civilization I
Greek	= Northeast Mediterranean civilization II
Roman	= Northeast Mediterranean civilization III
Byzantine	= Northeast Mediterranean civilization IV

The four would be phases of one localized continuum of civilization that lasted no longer than the continuity of China or India or Mesopotamia or Egypt. This interpretation has been developed in *Configurations* (pp. 687–695).

It is evident, I hope, that we are in the stage of seeing problems such as these, indeed of having them forced on the attention; even though our verdicts remain as undogmatic as possible.

In the face of these larger problems, let us then leave the question of when Western civilization will end, or whether it has already begun to end, and of how many stages, phases, or movements it will have consisted when it has terminated—let us leave these problematical matters to the future to which they belong. We can summarize our findings on the completed segments of Western civilization somewhat like this:

500/700–900±. Prodromal stage. Pre-national; Christianity still developing its root system; cultural patterns unformed.

900± — 1325±. First phase, Mediaeval. Nationalities present but little organized politically; culmination of Christianity; other culture, so far as well-patterned, saturated with Christianity.

1325± — 1575±. Transition, Renaissance in Italy; loosening and reconstitution of culture patterns in Transalpine Europe.

1575± — ?. Second phase, Modern. Nationalities politically organized; culture patterns founded on those of First phase but reformulated secularly, and of wider range.

? (1900?) — ?. Commencing disintegration of whole civilization? Or second transition to a third phase?

4. Flow and Reconstitution within Civilizations

THE FOLLOWING ANALYSIS is an endeavor of sorts in Applied Anthropology—a somewhat new kind of Applied Anthropology, of a long-range variety. It leans little on Economics or Sociology, but a great deal on History. Only it asks that History be viewed now and then with maximum of elbow room and freedom of perspective; with emphasis, for the time being, not on the mere events of History, which are as unending as the waves of the sea, but on its secular trends; and that these trends be construed so far as possible in terms of the stylelike patterns which so largely constitute civilizations, and of the developmental flow, interactions, and integration of these patterns.

I

I propose to examine how far civilizations possess each a set, direction, or slope which is bound up so closely with their intrinsic nature that it endures as long as the civilization lasts; or, on the contrary, how far the set or direction may change within a persisting civilization.

It is evident that this question implies the assumption that civilizations may be considered as really distinct, as legitimately separable.

In spite of the fact that all human cultures, primitive and advanced, possess a generic similarity of plan and continuity of oc-

---
Read at the Wenner-Gren Foundation, New York City, 1958.

currence, quite properly emphasized by anthropologists in certain connections; and in spite of the further fact that the major civilizations are all in some degree interconnected and interderivative, I nevertheless start from the premise that the civilizations of China, India, ancient Mesopotamia, Egypt, Graeco-Roman Antiquity, and our own Western civilization are sufficiently different from one another to make it profitable to treat them operationally as distinguishable and comparable units, each with qualities of its own sufficiently strong to justify our recognizing a particular set or direction, or over-all character, in each of the civilizations.

I propose also to understand civilizations as being each constituted—at least to a large extent—of a collection of styles. A style is first of all a self-consistent way of behaving or of doing things. A civilization, as the assemblage of the styles followed by the inhabitants of a certain area through a certain duration of time, would thus consist of a style or manner of government, added to a style of law, and another of social relations; further, a characteristic manner of production and economy, of religious belief and organization; plus what we ordinarily call its styles of literature, art, music, and building.

Within one civilization, its several styles not only coexist in the same society, region, and period; they also tend toward a certain consistency among themselves. If they were not interconsistent at first, as might well be the case, due to some of them having been introduced from the outside, they would nevertheless tend to become more consistent as they remained associated. Some degree of such consistency between the parts of civilizations has, I think, always been assumed for them; though often implicitly rather than expressly. And the assumption seems validated by the simple consideration that consistent and coherent civilizations would on the average work out better and get farther, and presumably survive longer, than inconsistent ones dragging on under malfunction and strain.

A civilization then can be said to possess a degree of consistency, or consonance, or accord in design, between its parts or ingredients; each of which parts in turn possesses a certain degree of unifiedly characteristic manner, way, or style.

II

We may now examine what we ordinarily call styles, such as styles in art, in institutions, or in dress, for their generic qualities or properties. After that, the question will arise whether the properties of styles adhere also to civilizations as style assemblages, or whether we must recognize new properties for them.

It is first necessary to distinguish *ways*, which, though sooner or later they change, are normally repetitive, from *styles* in the fuller sense of the word, where change is of their essence.

A manner of baking bread, of plowing a field, of laying brick, while certainly not foreordained, may nevertheless go on for centuries without material alteration, in one or more parts of the world. These are processes that tend toward the repetitively practical. By contrast, a fine art, a philosophy or a science, is creative. As long as it remains so, it is thereby prevented from repetitiousness. It tends first to develop and progress, later to degenerate and die. An art or a philosophy moves on; it cannot continue to spin on a pivot. Those more trivial styles which we call fashions, as in dress, change with particular rapidity. Not expressing or achieving much of intrinsic significance, they lack the full rise and fall, the consistent growth curve, of greater styles; but they are even more restless in the profile of their movement.

The more creative activities of civilizations thus are imbued with change in their very nature. To each activity there corresponds, at any given time, a style, a bundle of manners and qualities all its own. The style forms, develops, matures, decays, and either dissolves or atrophies into a dead petrifaction. The one thing it does not do is to stand still. Styles are the very incarnation of the dynamic process of history. They are the most sensitive expression extant of cultural change—its most delicate galvanometer.

As to the causes of styles, we know very little. The causes are obviously difficult to find. At best, we can do little more than describe the circumstances amid which a style forms. From there on, however, the story of the career of a style has unity. Its history usually possesses an internal self-consistency proportional to the definiteness of the style itself. A style definite in its themes, its manners, its affects, can be expected to run a definite course in successive stages, which we tend to describe in familiar terms like groping, growth of control, full power, slackening, dissolution; or again, as formative, developing, climactic, over-ripe, decadent.

I will say in passing that style histories characterizable in these terms are probably as typical of intellectual creativeness as of aesthetic. Philosophy and science tend to grow and behave, in the pattern of their normal careers, much like literature and the arts; though we are ordinarily less aware of the fact. There are several reasons for this lesser awareness—the cumulativeness of the aggregate products of science, for instance, and our modern bias for regarding the findings of science as constituting absolute and timeless truth. There is no leeway here to analyze these considerations, and my point will have to be accepted or rejected dogmatically, at least as regards science. However, it is obvious that throughout human history philosophy does arise and die away in stylistic spurts as do the arts.

Styles follow a recurrent pattern of growth. When we possess enough examples of an art, and adequate information as to the time sequence of its individual products, a newly discovered specimen within the style, an anonymous or hitherto unassigned one, can normally be dated within a half century, and often within a decade or two. This is possible through the specific quality of the piece in question, and through the recognized flow of successive qualities within the style. This ability of experts to agree in assigning its place in the style to any object, for example, Mediaeval sculpture, Renaissance and Modern painting, five or six centuries of European music, Greek vases and poetry, Chinese painting, is in a sense prediction: they predict what the date will turn out to be when all the facts are in. The whole procedure certainly implies that a style has a one-way course or life history.

Equally compelling as to the compulsive strength of style seen as a course is the long-recognized clustering of great men in time-limited constellations within each civilization or national sub-civilization. This clustering certainly is as conspicuously true for intellectual as for aesthetic creativeness. One can argue indefinitely here in a circle as to *cause*. Is it the greatness of geniuses that causes a style to come into being? Or does the growth of the style evoke successively greater geniuses until the culmination is reached—after which there is increasingly less left for talented individuals to do within the confines of the style? Yet as soon as we leave off the vain effort of tracking down the original or ultimate cause of the phenomenon of clustering, and concentrate on its recurrent generalized form or pattern, it is an indubitable fact that genius *occurs* preponderantly in conjunction with the developmental courses of outstanding styles within successful civilizations.

Now for any well-marked style, its course not only has a beginning and an end, but it is one-way. A true style does not travel so far and then retrace its steps; nor does it suddenly go off into a random new direction. The tendency is very strong for its direction not only to persevere up to a culmination, but to be irreversible. At its culmination, a style is utilizing its potentialities to their utmost. It really has no place left to go. Whether it nevertheless tries still to push ahead, or hesitates and stalls, its great achievements are over.

A bit of reflection shows that this quality of irreversibility is really implicit in most of our formulations of what style is, provided only we let ourselves conceive it as flowing in time, as it normally does flow.

It is because of this one-wayness of growth that we can speak of the history of a style as if it were a life history. It is also why a concrete exemplification taken from one style, such as Greek sculpture, or again Renaissance painting, of what is meant by terms like "archaic severity" or "primitive stiffness"; or by "increasing freedom of control" or "full liberation"—why such an illustration often suffices for us to recognize a corresponding stage of development in a wholly different art. Qualities such as flamboyant, over-ornate, Churrigueresque, Rococo, first defined as characteristic of particular developmental phases of Gothic and Renaissance architecture, can at times be applied with aptness to analogous phases in literatures, in decorative and applied arts, or in music. Again and again we find in diverse arts a similar course beginning with restraint, attaining balanced mastery, and ending in luxuriance, conscious emotionality, extremity, and disintegration.

This does not mean that there is any *absolute* level of, say, severity or exuberance or pathos that is characteristic of corresponding phases of different arts. One art may begin as emotionally as another ends. A dramatist just does deal with human emotions more directly and overtly than does an architect. We must therefore guard against inferring the place of an object within its style from the absolute degree of its restraint, emotion, luxuriance, etc. Its serial place will be assignable only on comparison *within* the style.

Only after styles in different civilizations are known as wholes, over their entire courses, does it become legitimate to compare their phases. Such an instance would be the comparison of late Greek Hellenistic literature with modern European literature. Both have behind them a tradition of mastery in dramatic, epic, and lyrical poetry; both have largely displaced verse by prose; both have become interested in realism and at the same time in subjectivism; both experiment in new forms without however succeeding in filling these with wholly satisfactory content. Such comparisons as this appear to have a certain genuine significance, but they can be made only after the phase-by-phase qualities of the compared styles have been ascertained independently.

In summary, we may say, then, that creative activities tend to appear in history in bursts which we call styles; that each style has a certain direction, uses particular methods or techniques, and achieves specific and more or less unique qualities; that that is why every style possesses a significant internal consistency or coherence; and why the course of the style, its life history, contains, because of this coherence, at least an element or considerable degree of irreversibility.

III

Let us now proceed to our second problem, namely to examine how far the special stylistic quality of irreversibility attaches also to civilizations, which, as we have seen, may from one angle be considered as more or less coherent associations of styles; or how far whole civilizations, which are much larger phenomena than styles, possess special properties that may leave room for reversibility, or at least for divertibility of direction.

The idea of "direction" is fundamental in this inquiry, because we are examining civilizations not as static entities but as limited processes of flow in time. Greek civilization is a good archetypal example of civilizations and their flow: it was sharply characterized, high in creative power, brief in duration; to an unusual degree, almost all the activities of Greek civilization culminated nearly simultaneously, at least overlappingly, within a mere three centuries. Its course is therefore particularly like that of a style, unrolling like the consistent plot of a drama, inevitable and irreversible. And irreversibility, whether of entropy in physics or of human destiny, carries implications of fate and doom.

It is evident that Spengler's system of declines and extinctions —his "Untergang" means literally a "sinking"—was derived basically from a contrastive comparison of Greek civilization with European or Western civilization. And as this latter is still a going concern, his idea of the pessimistic fate and extinction awaiting it was evidently taken over from what had happened to Graeco-Roman civilization.

However, let us go a step farther. Spengler assumes as something that does not need to be argued—and so does Toynbee—a larger Graeco-Roman civilization. Spengler calls this larger unit that Greek culture and Roman culture were but the two halves of

Classical Antiquity—"die Antike"; and Toynbee calls it simply Hellenic civilization. Historians also often group the two together as "Ancient History," as against Mediaeval-Modern History which deals largely with other peoples in another part of Europe in a subsequent period. There is excellent warrant for joining Greek and Roman achievements into the one larger unity because the contributions of the two complemented each other so thoroughly. The Greeks' strength lay in aesthetic and intellectual creativity. Here the Romans were poor imitators, except for literature, and even in that they were admittedly derivative. On the other hand, the energetic, passionate, unstable Greeks were weak on the executive side, in substantial accomplishment. In empire, administration, law, and engineering the Romans did what the Greeks in part tried but performed inadequately, in part did not even attempt. It is this close supplementing of Greeks and Romans in achievement, as well as in population, area, and period, that validates including them both in a single major civilization. Half the Roman Empire spoke Greek as its cultural if not official language; and it was this Greek half that survived—still calling itself Roman, though we say "Byzantine"—for a thousand years after the "fall of the Roman empire" in 476—really the fall only of its Roman half.

The next step brings us to the period often loosely called the Dark Ages, the interval between Ancient and Mediaeval times. This is the period of Goths, Lombards, Saxons, and Franks; of decay of government, arts, letters, and wealth; a time when our Western civilization had not yet begun to crystallize out but the Imperial Roman days and ways were irretrievably over. It was a time definitely of cultural retreat, of decay both quantitative and qualitative; not a separate civilization as such but a chaotic, amorphous interregnum between civilizations. Here we do find seeming reversibility, or at least reversal of a sort: a heavy sag of cultural level, a sag alike in the economic, organizational, and creative level.

But what does this reversion turn out to be? It proves to be the disintegration of the patterns of one civilization, a very decomposition of its substance and form. And at the same time there are dim stirrings, blind gropings, the germinating seeds from which Western civilization will begin to grow within a few centuries.

In short, our Dark Ages are not really a reversal, a retracing, of a current of flow. They mark the cessation of flow of one civilization; a consequent slack water and hesitation of confused fluctuating drift; and then the gradual and slowly increasing flow of the new Western civilization—new precisely because the set of its current is in a new direction.

Our slump, the Dark Age, accordingly is the falling apart and dissolution of most of an old civilization, because of which dissolution a new civilization was able to arise—and move in a new direction.

The largest single active constituent which the Ancient Mediterranean civilization and Western civilization shared was Christianity; though this was a disruptive force in Rome and a strong constructive one in the later West. Spengler, compulsively bent on exaggerating genuine qualitative differences into absolute separateness and total incompatibility, could not let two civilizations, each of which he felt as monadal, share anything consequential. So he invented a Magian or Syro-Arabian civilization to which he could ascribe the origin of Christianity as something consonant in spirit. This Magian civilization of Spengler is a subtle and intriguing—or irritating—concoction, but it corresponds to only tenuous historical reality.

Toynbee also saw a challenge in the fact that Christianity was shared by two distinct civilizations. His response was the devising of a generic mechanism: the religion that serves as a chrysalis in which one civilization—a fully mature larva, so to speak—pupates in order to reëmerge after a time in the bright imago of a new though affiliated civilization. Christianity is his best example, and his generic mechanism of the chrysalis is evidently built upon its case. However, he cites several other instances which carry varying degrees of conviction.

Among these, his second best case is probably Buddhism as it became established in China between A.D. 200 and 600 and as it serves to separate China of the Shang, Chou, and Han dynasties, which he calls the "Sinic" civilization, from China of T'ang, Sung, and Ming, or the "Main Far Eastern" civilization. For simplicity's sake we may name them China I and China II. The four intervening centuries, between these two, did not sag as deeply, probably, as the corresponding ones in Europe; but they were a time of some confusion and breakdown, including conquests by foreigners and civil war between rival dynasties. China I had evolved a distinctive philosophy, a literature, sculpture, an empire, and an administrative system. China II produced Neo-Confucian philosophy, a distinctive algebra, poetry with new themes and new meters, a style of sculpture different from the old, and a highly characteristic style of painting, as well as a series of original institutions, such as a civil-service examination system in place of feudalism. That Buddhism was the cause of these innovations would be hard to prove. Toynbee does not try to prove it. He merely says that the four centuries of establishment of Buddhism were the chrysalis in which China II grew until it could hatch out.

Now China I and II seem considerably less differentiated, all in all, than Ancient Mediterranean is from Western civilization. This may be the result of the two Chinese periods continuing attached mainly to the same soil, whereas the Ancient and Western civilizations shared only about a quarter of their territories—Italy, Spain, France. On the whole perhaps most of us fail to separate China I and China II into two separate civilizations because most of us do not know enough about either; and the Sinologists do not because the native Chinese historians do not. Nevertheless, it does seem practically certain that there is less making of basically new patterns, less new total direction, as between China I and II, and more preserved continuity, all in all, than between the Ancient and Western cultures.

Whereas Toynbee has proposed recognizing two successive civilizations in China, he keeps Egypt as a single civilization. Yet the Egyptologists have long dealt with the equivalent of what might be called Egypt I, II, III, IV: or, as they name them, Old

Kingdom, Middle Kingdom, New Empire, Renascence. These are separated by interregna of civil war, confusion, poverty, great slumps in architecture and art. All intervals between periods, except the first interval, also involve invasions and conquests by foreigners. No one, not even Toynbee, proposes to view the four successive cultural pulses or beats in Egypt as constituting four civilizations: they are too much alike. They are alike in spite of a fair amount of gradual innovation due both to seepage of import from abroad and to home inventiveness. The art, the hieroglyphic writing, most of the religion, the empire itself, all kept much the same forms through periods I and II and III and IV. When they finally died out it was because Persian conquest, and Greek, Roman, and Christian forces of acculturation, had slowly gnawed away all native Egyptian elements of culture. The civilization grew too feeble to defend itself in a more vigorous world and was slowly eaten up piecemeal.

It is clear from these instances in the West, in China, and in Egypt, that to understand better the behavior and therefore the presumable destinies of civilizations, their life histories and deaths, we are still in need of a sharper comprehension of what constitutes the boundaries of a civilization, a better empirical definition of what delimits one civilization as distinct from another one. Too few people have really thought about this, fewer still have tried to validate their conclusions with sufficient historical evidence.

IV

Let us probe a bit into a specific problem, and one that applies to ourselves today.

Many besides Spengler have noticed the parallel between the contemporary phase of our civilization and the Hellenistic-Early Imperial phase of Classical Antiquity, which we have already touched upon as regards their literatures. The period in question runs from say 200 B.C. to A.D. 200, from soon after Alexander the Great to the Antonine Emperors in Rome. In these phases of both civilizations, the Graeco-Roman and our own, rural life recedes; urbanization proceeds apace; wealth multiplies, great civilian fortunes are acquired. The population is mobile and floating, people of many nationalities jostle one another in metropolises, provincial dialects disappear. A multitude of free cities and small states has been replaced by fewer and fewer great powers. Luxuries and conveniences abound, but are also out of reach of a proletariat. Public buildings rise on an unheard-of scale, but architecture emphasizes mass or splendor instead of proportion. Sculpture and painting imitate the great masters of the past, or go in for the bizarre, or the realistically commonplace, or the exaggerated, in order to be new. Literature shows the same characteristics, as we have already set forth. Philosophy repeats the ideas of previous centuries.

Granted the parallel, or its prevailing cogency, the question naturally arises: Will the parallel continue? Is there awaiting us a period like that which followed A.D. 200 in Mediterranean lands? A period of civil war, of economic contraction; a breakdown of skills and standards along with security and order, while aesthetic and intellectual originality and creativity sink to the vanishing point; until the total civilization has disintegrated, with the barbarians moving in to take over.

This subsequent breakdown is, in the large, what happened in Antiquity from A.D. 200 to 500 after the Hellenistic-Early Imperial age that seems so like our own days. Must we then project, by analogy, the same curve, a similar fate, for ourselves from 1950 to 2200 or 2300? Spengler was sure we must. Toynbee thinks we can escape, but only by moral character. Millions, without being aware of the parallel, dimly wonder at the portents of our days, or worry out loud.

I shall keep out of prophecy, but try to analyze the analogy, to dissect the seemingly deadly parallel.

Of all analogues to our contemporary civilization, the late Graeco-Roman Empire period of Ancient Mediterranean civilization does seem the closest. But this is partly due to the fact that we know it far better than we know China or Egypt, India or Mesopotamia. We see more parallels just because knowledge is far richer.

Next there is the fact of the definite kinship of Graeco-Roman and our civilization. They are in a sense mother and daughter. The two have always overlapped in area. They almost abut in time. And we have of course inherited, have bodily taken over, a large part of our cultural stock-in-trade from the parental Mediterranean civilization: Christianity, our alphabet, much of our speech, philosophy, and law, the fundamentals of technology, to name only a few of our legacies. Therefore we cannot fairly assume that all of our surface similarity to late Helleno-Roman civilization is symptomatic of a parallel *stage* of decay and impending death. Much of the similarity of our civilization has always characterized it as a result of its derivation.

But why should not the Western world's present tensions, wars, realignments, rapid changes, and distresses be construed with equal likelihood as the growing pains of a *reconstitution* such as China experienced around 200 to 600, and Egypt several times?—instead of being construed as the final dissolution of a civilization coming down with the crash of a Götterdämmerung?

Our own civilization has in fact already experienced one reconstitution. With the Graeco-Roman civilization essentially dead, in the West, around A.D. 500, its still surviving patterns disintegrated still more for some centuries thereafter. Christianity, though established, was still too new, too nearly illiterate and undisciplined, to have yet evolved its new patterns of creativity which it did evolve later. The Dark Ages following 500 were dark not only because of ignorance but because people had lost the old patterns and not yet evolved new ones of any definiteness or moment. This absence of Dark Age patterns, due to previous ones having dissolved away, and new ones having not yet formed, is the symptom that most marks off Ancient from Western civilization. The nexus of patterns and values in Europe after the Dark Age interregnum was, all in all, more different from the nexus existing before, during Graeco-Roman Antiquity, than it was similar. We have here, incidentally, a tentative, empirical definition of what a civilization is, what sets one off from another: it is an excess of distinctive patterns, values, or directions over shared ones.

Some time after Charlemagne, around 900 or 950, the new Western civilization emerged. Compared with the vague stirrings of its germination in the preceding dark centuries, it now emerged with definite form however rude and in need of further development. It manifested several patterns that were to continue in its structure thereafter. First of all, the new civilization was unmitigatedly committed to being Christian. There was no room in it for anything else in the domain of religion; and its Christianity was unified. Second, the European nationalities had pretty definitely crystallized out by 900 or 950, much as they were to endure for a thousand years. There were now Frenchmen, Germans, Italians, Englishmen, Danes, Poles replacing tribal agglomerations or the loose Frankish Empire of Charlemagne. These nationalities found political expression in feudalistic monarchies. Fortified castles were rising, and in their lee, or within their own walls, towns grew up—still puny but a beginning toward urban life. Romanesque-Gothic building got under way, and then the associated sculpture and stained glass. A revival of learning had commenced—still very modest but to bear fruit within a century in the first pulse of Scholastic philosophy. Much in the same way, the writing of vernacular tongues—French instead of Latin—also emerged in the 900's, proceeded to poetical compositions in the 1000's, and culminated in the vernacular Mediaeval literatures—French, Provençal, Castilian, and German—in the 1100's and 1200's.

This civilization here arising was Western Civilization; but it was Western Civilization in its High Mediaeval phase or stage. It came to a conspicuous peak—its Christianity and church, its monarchies, its architecture and sculpture, its thought—in the mid-thirteenth century: let us say in the decades around 1250. In fact, the "Summa" of St. Thomas Aquinas in 1265 may be construed as the literal summation, formal and inward, of the High Middle Ages.

Now, if this Mediaeval civilization of Western Europe had reached its thirteenth-century peak and then begun to decline, and had withered away without issue, it would nevertheless have been, in and by itself, a respectable civilization: not one of the greatest, but a good second-rank civilization, comparable for instance to that of the Mohammedan Arabs; and equally set apart and distinctive.

This High Mediaeval civilization did not wither away. Instead, its patterns loosened and partly dissolved, during the two centuries or so following 1300. But as they broke down they were also *reconstituting* themselves, and on an ampler scope. This went on until, at some time between 1500 and 1600, the filling in of these newly enlarged patterns, the actualization of their now greater potential, had got under way: and therewith "Modern History" began—the history of the second or Modern phase of Western Civilization.

What confronted west Europeans around 1300 or 1325, though they did not of course see it in the perspective of subsequent history, was an alternative. They might either adhere to their patterns of High Mediaeval civilization as they had first begun to rough them out four centuries before, and had since filled them in and realized them so successfully. In that case, the saturation of the patterns having been essentially achieved, life under the continuing culture would have become increasingly repetitive, creativity would have been checked, atrophy ensued, and an irrevocable withering of the Mediaeval civilization would have got under way. The other choice was for the Europeans of 1300 to stretch their cultural patterns to accommodate a civilization of larger scope: to stretch them if necessary until some of them burst; to stretch them by stuffing into them a content of far greater knowledge of fact, more experimentation and curiosity, wider horizons, greater wealth, a higher standard of living.

They took the risk of this second course. They did stretch their patterns of living a civilized life, they ruptured many of them, they developed more new ones in their place; until, after two to three centuries, the set of patterns, the over-all design for living, had been reconstituted, and a new stage of Western civilization, the Modern stage, was entered upon.

High Mediaeval civilization was like its cathedrals of high-reared arches but narrow base. What it lacked seems almost incredible today—at least it seems incredible that Mediaeval men —our ancestors and the founders of our civilization of today— could have been complacent about it. There was no active science whatever. Scholastic philosophy was competent, but only within a framework of authority set in advance. Mediaeval architecture is unrivaled, but only for religious purposes. There developed an original sculpture, but no true free painting. Literature lacked both drama and prose. In technology there was the beginning of some traceable advance over Antiquity in the use of mills and natural power, but still on a provincial scale only. Mediaeval transportation remained rudimentary, wealth astonishingly small —the first gold coins in Western Europe were minted only as late as 1252. Cities were pitifully tiny, and filthy. Food was monotonous, the comforts of life rude, luxuries of the meagerest. The known world consisted of part of Europe with one extension line to Constantinople and Jerusalem—and the Mongols now and then incalculably bursting in from the unknown.

As against this contented parochialism of High Mediaevalism the 1300's, 1400's, and 1500's brought first a wider knowledge of Asia, next of the African peripheries, then of America. Trade followed, industry grew, wealth expanded. A true civilian architecture arose in Italy; painting blossomed beside sculpture. The hold of the Church—into which so many of the High Mediaeval patterns had ramified—this hold was loosened or broken. The papacy was dragged to Avignon, then split in the Great Schism; councils were held to heal the breach and—unsuccessfully—to combat the worldliness and profligacy of churchmen, a worldliness that in turn was building up sentiments of anticlericalism, and the dissidency of Wycliffe and Hus. Not long afterward, the Reformation tore away from the hitherto unified Church nearly half of Europe.

All this was certainly a process of disintegration of what had been well fitted and firm in the true Middle Ages. In philosophy, the Scholastic system was similarly disrupted by the skeptical negativism of Occam or dissolved into mysticism by the Germans —after which its field lay fallow. Science, after a thousand years' sleep, was slow to reconstitute itself. Toward the end of our period of readjustment, it finally got into motion with Copernicus's 1543 revolution of astronomy, and with contemporary Italian discoveries in mathematics and medicine. Printing was invented to meet the demands for more knowledge and ideas on the part of a greatly enlarged civilian and urban clientele of sharpening curiosity.

In many ways this era of Reconstitution and Rebirth between the Mediaeval and Modern periods of Western Civilization must have felt to the people of Europe much as the twentieth century feels to us. It was a period of strains and unsettlement. The timorous must often have wondered if the world were not coming wholly out of joint. True, such sentiment must also have been felt in some degree in the Dark Ages. The difference is that the Dark Ages *were* an actual recession: there just was less civilization, quantitatively and qualitatively, in the pit of their sag than there was before and after. Contrariwise, 1400 and 1500 were not true recessions or sags but times of growth along with reconstitution, of advance accompanied by reorientation. There was more knowledge in 1400 and 1500 than before, increased understanding and cultivation, more urbane living, and greater wealth. Growth, not recession, continued through the interval, even while the reconstitution of structure was taking place. That, incidentally, is why no one has yet proposed separating the Middle Ages off from the Modern period as being two distinct civilizations. Their respective sets or directions were altered and enlarged in the period of Reconstitution; but they were not wholly torn apart, nor was there loss or destruction of most of what had existed in Western Civilization I—the Middle Ages— during the Reconstitution into Western Civilization II—Modern Europe.

Our 1300–1550 period of Reconstitution evidently corresponds fairly to the Chinese 200-600 in being a time of unsettlement and reorientation after which the civilization resumed its course on a reorganized and broadened base. Therefore it seems more fitting to recognize these two Chinese phases also as China I and II, or as Ancient China and Mediaeval-Modern China, than as two disparate civilizations separated even by their names as Toynbee proposes.

There is one interesting difference from Europe, however: China acquired a new organized religion, Buddhism, in its era of Reconstitution; Europe loosened the hold of Christianity, especially as organized in the Church.

It is even clearer that I, II, III, IV of Egypt could have been no more than phases of one civilization, as has always been assumed. Each phase regularly returned to nearly everything the preceding one had had. The interims were times of disorganization, followed by reorganization; but without serious broadening of scope, or reorientation, or reconstitution on a new design.

Toward the end of Egypt III, it is true, there was an effort to reach a new outlook, to formulate a new design—with monotheism, a "truthful" art, a new writing. But this effort originated from above; it failed, and was not renewed. This is not the place to dissect this interesting attempt to which the name Ikhnaton is attached. The episode does seem to fit, and thus to confirm, our working theory of the relation of civilizations to the setting, reconstitution, or disintegration of their over-all patterns.

V

Let us recapitulate our argument.

The characteristic forms of culture which are non-repetitive, plastic, and creative, are its styles. Styles are characterized first by internal consistency; second by the property of growth; and third, by a quality of irreversibility: they can develop but they cannot "disdevelop" or turn back. All three of these qualities—consistency, growth, and irreversibility—are characteristic also of organisms; though this similarity is only analogous, since organisms are animals or plants functioning through physiology and heredity, whereas styles are social products of the one species of organism, man.

Civilizations contain more or less repetitive elements in which the qualities of style are present only feebly or transiently; but they not only do also contain styles, but on their creative dynamic side they consist characteristically of styles. They may be described accordingly as a collocation or association of styles; and in proportion as this association is integrated, we can usefully regard a civilization as a sort of superstyle, or master style, possessing some degree of over-all design and being set, faced, or sloped in a specific and more or less unique direction.

A civilization would presumably partake of the qualities of the styles of which it is composed. Besides the consistency or coherence which we have just mentioned, civilizations should then show also the property of growth; and this property they are indeed generally credited with. Finally, civilizations might share with styles the property of irreversibility; and this is the problem we have set ourselves to inquire into.

There are well-defined civilizations, such as the ancient Egyptian, which have dissolved away and sooner or later have been replaced by others. As integrated entities, they have long been what we popularly call them: dead. We may describe their death as due to the exhaustion of the potentialities in the superstyle which is the most significant part of a civilization. This would be construed as analogous to the ultimate exhaustion, within any particular creative style, of the potentialities to which it is committed in virtue of being a style. With its creativity exhausted, a civilization is either taken over and absorbed and thus replaced by another; or its patterns as well as its styles dilapidate, crumble, and collapse into confusion. Such periods in which processes of disorganization prevail over constructive organization are like the interregnum called the Dark Ages which followed Graeco-Roman civilization and preceded our own Western civilization.

We have reviewed and on the whole confirmed the similarity alleged between the post-culmination condition of Graeco-Roman civilization of 200 B.C. to A.D. 200 and the contemporary condition of our own, with its growing sense of crisis, and in some quarters fear of doom. In ancient times this condition was followed from A.D. 200 to 500 by increasing collapse of cultural patterns and organization, further followed, from 500 to about 900, by the Dark Age of amorphous chaos of civilization in Western Europe. Another collapse and Dark Age may therefore seem to loom ahead for us.

However, an alternative parallel or analogue is furnished by the period of Reconstitution which Western civilization underwent from about 1300 to 1550, after the style patterns of its High Mediaeval Phase had been exhausted, and from which its Modern Phase emerged with reorientation and a broadened set of patterns. This period of Reconstitution—of which the Renaissance was one part—was also a time of strain, conflict, crisis, uncertainties, and loosening of patterns. However, population, wealth, curiosity, knowledge, enterprise, and invention continued to grow during the period. These advances were concurrent with the dissolution of the exhausted Mediaeval style patterns; with the result that new sets of patterns were being evolved as the worn-out ones were being abandoned; and thus a second phase of Western civilization was successfully launched. The contrast with the Graeco-Roman course of events is that there the exhaustion and breakdown of style patterns was accompanied not by expansion but by contraction of population, wealth, curiosity, knowledge, enterprise, and invention. Thus the critical period became one of Collapse instead of Reconstitution.

When now we match the present condition of our civilization comparatively against these two analogues, it seems fairly clear that the correspondence is greater with the European stage of Reconstitution than with the Graeco-Roman stage of Dissolution. This is because now, as in 1300–1550, population, wealth, curiosity, knowledge, enterprise, and invention are definitely still in an expanding phase. It seems somewhat likely, accordingly, that we are now in the throes of a second stage of Reconstitution of our civilization. In that case, period Western Civilization II would already be mainly past, whether we so recognize it or not, and period Western Civilization III lies ahead of us whenever we shall have finished reorganizing our cultural style patterns with a resultant new over-all set or direction.

Of course all historical prediction, or even contemporary diagnosis, must remain approximate and tentative, since correspondences are never wholly parallel in history, and since it is of the nature of history to show analogies while disguising any homologies it may contain. Still, the preponderance of correspondence does seem to be as set forth, so that we may reasonably incline toward the inference that it is the symptoms of a stage of major reconstitution that are alarming us.

5. Periodization

SOME INTERESTING PARALLELS developed to problems with which anthropologists deal, especially in archaeology, at a session in the 1954 annual meeting in New York City of the American Historical Association, which was devoted to "Criteria of Periodization in History" under the chairmanship of Geoffrey Bruun.

D. Gerhard pointed out that the prevalent division of political history into Ancient, Mediaeval, and Modern was preceded by an older one in which periodization was on the basis of a succession of empires—Assyrian, Persian, Greek, Roman, and Holy Roman. Even within the last two centuries there has been some fluctuation of choice of events used to signalize the beginnings of the Mediaeval and Modern eras. As for the "Contemporary" subdivision of the latter, Gerhard pointed out that the custom of initiating this with the French Revolution was open to the objection that 1789 marked the break-through into overt effect of ideological causes operative throughout the preceding century of increasing enlightenment. He favored, therefore, a primary classification of European history into a prologue preceding 1000, a first stage of 1000 to 1200, a second of 1200 to 1700, the third from 1700 on. This scheme of course throws together into one major period the High Middle Ages, the Renaissance, the Reformation, and the Religious Wars; but nevertheless the period is held together by certain principles and directions—corporate

---

MS written in 1954.

organization, or enlightenment, for example. But the recognition and use of principles and directions means moving away from pure *events* which constitute the primary raw material of history toward *trends*, toward generalizations which discover and define *culture patterns*.

It is also obvious that American archaeology has had its parallel to the obsolete historical method of periodizing by empire successions: Toltec-Aztec, Old-New Maya (where the "empire" was as forced as in the case of Greek ascendancy). Peruvian pre-history also experienced a phase of recognizing Megalithic, Tiahuanaco, and Inca empires. Yet Peruvian tradition was so meager compared with Meso-American that its hold was soon broken, and our modern Formative, Florescent, Fusional, and Imperial (or Cultist, Experimental, Master Craftsman, Expansionist, City Building, and Imperialist) phases aim to denote representative cultural stages rather than successive repetition phases of political dominance.

H. Heaton, speaking of periodizing in economic history, made clear that like general anthropology this study began with setting up stages of an orderly evolution. This effort was succeeded by a centering on economic "systems" or types, such as feudal, capitalist, etc., most of which, however inadequate, at least dealt with a spatio-temporal historic continuity.

Meyer Schapiro, treating art history, agreed with the other speakers that many different periodizations were valid, and new ones would continue to be proposed, the aim being not to achieve the impossible of an ultimate and absolute classification, but to attain to more and more meaningful ones.

In the field of art, he said, the first delimitations were dynastic, such as Carolingian, Ottonian, etc. Next came designations by periods that were at least more or less cultural, such as Renaissance; and finally those by stylistic concepts like Baroque, though some of the earlier of these, such as Romanesque and Gothic, rested upon plain historical error, and all of them have tended to shift meaning with continued use. Finally, these stylistic concepts were extended to other arts and even to non-aesthetic domains of culture, as when one speaks of Baroque music or Baroque philosophy.

Schapiro went on to say that the products of an art period are similar not only in manner but in recurring close together in space and time. This in turn means that a natural group of works of art can be mapped in a spatio-temporal matrix, and possesses typical qualities. These qualities constitute its inner essence, and cannot be accounted for by contemporary or antecedent events of a political, economic, or non-aesthetic nature. Causes can be sought more or less successfully for the events of history, but hardly for its styles.

I agree with this finding and believe it must be accepted. *De facto* it is generally if tacitly accepted by art historians; also by archaeologists. One style can influence another, and such phenomena of contact and derivation are of course noted, and traced by archaeologists and historians of art; for instance the impingement of Greek on northwest Indian Gandhara sculpture in the early Christian centuries. But such cases can be viewed as extensions of one style at the expense of another. In any event the phenomena remain on the stylistic level. What is apparently extremely difficult is to determine with reliability non-stylistic causes for a style. This means that styles are relatively autonomous —somewhat as are languages. The essential qualities of any one style are interrelated, linked by an inherent coherence, which is also a "pattern" in the stricter sense, a gestalt or configuration. It is this inherent coherence that gives to a true style its relative imperviousness to influences from outside; though the imperviousness is never absolute, and seemingly is more readily influenced by other styles than by any non-stylistic pressures or exposures.

Form and content can be distinguished in style. Form involves first of all a technique; and this results in a certain kind of appearance of the finished product, such as rhyme or cire-perdu bronze casting or pointillism or water color or musical accompaniment. The technique is where external factors enter and influence a style: through a technology, an instrument, a repetitive formula of sound pattern such as refrain or meter. The forms achieved by such techniques also serve as means of achieving certain ends. These ends constitute the content of the works produced in a certain style. When the means themselves become an end of the production, the role of the content is correspondingly diminished, and virtuosity, in the adverse sense of the word, holds increasing sway.

The content of an art product is also called its subject or theme. It is the story or action, the melody, the person or act or thing represented. The content exercises its appeal by virtue of an affect, a mood or feeling tone, which it evokes. This mood can be pervasive and sustained or concentrated and variable; but it is probable that we value or rate a work of art partly on the strength of the affect evoked and partly according to the congeniality or compatibility of the affect with our momentary or temperamental background of mood.

When it comes to the matter of representation, the arts differ among themselves. Literature, whose technical medium is words, which in their nature have meaning as well as sound pattern, is under almost complete necessity to give primacy to representation of nature, persons, acts, or feelings. Music, on the other hand, operates with sounds that carry no semantic significance in themselves, but have strong visceral and kinaesthetic appeal. Its "themes" accordingly do not "represent" anything in nature but are almost pure gestalt interrelations of elements non-significant alone, but which together directly evoke affect, response, emotion. The visual arts range all the way from avowedly representational to avowedly non-representational effects, the choice depending variably on technology and material, skill, use of the product, and many other factors. Under some circumstances, such as limited technique or skill, an abbreviated, allusive representation may elicit more aesthetic response than an ambitiously full one. But this does not mean that subordination of theme to technique—such as "story" to brush stroke in a painting—is in itself a virtue.

Similar affects can be produced by different themes, or different affects by very similar themes. Witness the Davids of Donatello, Michaelangelo, Bernini. This suggests that it may be more rewarding to recognize three principal aspects of works of art: technique, theme, affect, rather than only the two of form and content. "Form" is especially liable to ambiguity. Literally, the form achieved is produced by the technique, expresses and therewith makes the theme what it is, and this in turn is the chief element that elicits affect.

It is probable that no style is ever wholly static. Some flow or movement is of its essence, though this may be rapid or very slow. In principle, styles are therefore irreversible. In so far as this is so, particular works of art can be defined by their locus on the curve or profile of development of the style. The same applies to artists, though their active lives would each cover a segment or span rather than a point.

However, styles do sometimes interpenetrate and fuse, they develop in pulses, phases, or substyles, they sometimes seem to be completing their course but then reconstitute themselves, they can fall on evil days along with their culture and wither prematurely, and so on. Their flow and irreversibility must therefore be looked upon as a limiting principle and not as a literal and factual universality.

So far as styles are relatively autonomous, they can be viewed as growths springing from immanent forces. But as the autonomy is never absolute, the immanence is never complete, and must not be sought or pursued back beyond the formation of the style.

With the shrinkage and fusion of our earth during the spurt of the last century and especially in recent decades, and the enormous part mechanisms of reproduction, preservation, communication, translation, and the like now play, the natural history of styles in the future may be quite different from that of the past. We now have in our consciousness, or at least in our simultaneous reach, knowledge of many of the styles developed by man throughout culture, instead of being under the dominance of one only at a time in each field, with only minor infringement by occasional competitors. It is accordingly possible that we may hereafter be working aesthetically from an accumulative fund or international pool of styles, much as science operates, into larger coördinations of a new kind of style. This possibility is supported by the fact that while the course of science as a whole has been accumulative while art has not, nevertheless the particular historic growths of science and philosophy have tended to come in pulses or bursts each characterized by some stylelike coherence of direction and quality.

There already are visible symptoms of such multiple style influencings. Picasso's painting in three or four styles as distinct as his neo-classic, cubist, double-vision fauve, and symbolic manners seems a case in point; especially as these manners are highly contrastive and not phases of a development in one direction; also in that the manners are not successive, but alternatingly resumed. Picasso's multiple style is unique in the history of art, in a painter of his sensitivity, imagination, and execution. The intermittent reaching back to snatches of allusion or quotation from the past in the poetry of Pound and Eliot—a sort of double tight-rope walking—may be allied; or again possibly it is only a special case of the wavering which is characteristic of the exhaustion phase of a style—regressive archaizing impulses occurring alongside forward disintegrative ones. But the lifelong multiple-personality styles of Picasso do seem an indubitably new phenomenon and perhaps precursor of more to come.

6. The Role of Style in Comparative Civilizations

I. Nature and Range of Style

THE FOLLOWING is an effort to see how far the concept of style can profitably be applied to the concept of civilizations viewed as wholes.

A style may be provisionally defined as a system of coherent ways or patterns of doing certain things.

The derivation of the word style is of course from stylus, the ancient writing tool, used metaphorically to express the individual manner peculiar to a writer. Just as there are individual handwritings and we might speak of idioscripts, so we have recognizable individual ways of expression in words, which were what were first called styles.

From literary composition the term was extended into the other arts, where terms such as brush or chisel, or touch on a musical instrument, might just as well have been employed.

So far, we have the original meaning attaching to the word style; and this meaning with reference to individuals has never died out. In addition, however, with lapse of time the word style has come also to denote a social or historical phenomenon, the manner or set of related patterns common to the writers or musicians or painters of a period and country.

Read before the Comparative Civilizations Symposium at the Center for Advanced Study in the Behavioral Sciences, Stanford, California, spring, 1958.

With the growth of historical interest in the wider sense, of a feeling for historicity in human phenomena, the extended sociocultural sense of the word style has grown; until today the word style is used in this social or historic sense perhaps more often than in the personal and individual one.

An extended use of the term is found in archaeology, in the investigation of cultures whose remains are not accompanied by inscriptions in writing, so that classifications and recognition of changes have to be made from visible, objective criteria. In such a situation objects whose shape is not predetermined by their use, and which maintain a certain plasticity of form or ornament within their range of manner, are often of great value in the determination of successive periods in the same culture—or for that matter of the irruption of other cultures into an existing one. Pottery of course, with its extreme plasticity, is a particularly striking example of a medium in which even minor stylistic changes can be assuredly recognized. It tends to be almost imperishable. It is made of material which originally is soft and therefore susceptible of a great variety of shapes and surface treatment. Pottery is usually abundant, if it occurs at all, and even fragments may bear characteristic qualities of a style. Consequently, in a number of areas, as in preliterate Japan or in Peru, sequences of culture periods have been worked out—primarily by the recognition of related but distinct pottery styles, each characterizing either an area or a period or both. In such instances the recognition of sociocultural styles has become an initiating tool for unraveling or discovering predocumentary culture history. Not of course that the recognition of pottery styles is sufficient to describe the entire culture. But pottery has often been the part of the culture in which stylistic quality was most markedly and abundantly observable in the surviving remains, and has therefore been used as a line of exploration through the successive changes of the culture: a line of discovery to which subsequently less abundant or less coherent facts brought to light by excavation could be attached—finally with firm assurance of representing a true historic sequence.

The recognition and determination of cultural styles is therefore a mechanism for delimiting, characterizing, and organizing historically related cultural phenomena. Such operating with styles for culture-historical purposes is, on the one hand, a way of differentiating or discriminating where discrimination is profitable for historical understanding. On the other hand it is also a help in bridging from one style to another, and in uniting styles intrinsically, or temporally, or geographically.

In the nature of things, the archaeological techniques of recovery cannot be extended outright to other aesthetic products which leave no visible traces. These usually must wait upon historic record. But where the historic record is full enough, the styles of all arts become accepted as significant of cultural development.

From the fine arts the concept of style can be carried over into the "public" arts of ritual and religion, and into the domestic arts of decoration, dress fashion, gastronomy, etc. We are here entering areas of culture which are at least partly involved in subsistence and survival and protocol, but yet an indubitable element of style is also present.

In all the fine arts it is apparent that the factor of style enters equally whatever the medium used. Music and sculpture, drama and dance, poetry and prose, are all equally subject to being organized in terms of styles.

What all fine arts share in addition to being subject to style, or always executed in a style, is an element which for want of a better and established term may be called creativity. It might be said of style that it is the manner in which creativity expresses itself; or, turning the phrase around, that creativity necessarily presupposes and produces a style.

While creativity is on the one hand aesthetic, it is at other times intellectual, in the larger sense. The world in general recognizes both aesthetic and intellectual creativity as hallmarks of "higher culture," and as expressive of the values attained by cultures.

The fact of this doubleness of creativity raises the suspicion whether the concept of style may not be legitimately applicable to intellectual creativity. While such an idea may seem far-fetched at first, it is at least supported by the fact that historical occurrences of intellectual and aesthetic creativity resemble each other in that both tend to come in more or less discontinuous pulses or spurts, and that they are marked by unusual frequency, or clustering, of individuals to whom we ascribe the quality of genius.

This historic parallelism of aesthetic and intellectual creativity is superficially disguised by the fact that the products of intellectual creativity seem to link together more continuously, and to accumulate much more, than do the products of aesthetic creativity. There is an old saying that science goes on through the ages and piles up, whereas the arts have always to begin over again. While this may be largely true so far as ultimate results are concerned, yet when we transfer attention from results to creativity itself, from products to productivity, it appears that the occurrences of pure science have been as discontinuous in history, and as seemingly irregular and spasmodic, as those in the fine arts. Behaviorally, therefore, there is historic justification for treating the two sorts of activities as alike, up to a certain point, and it becomes legitimate to inquire into the recognition of style in intellectual creativity.

The alleged cumulativeness of science is, as a matter of fact, largely restricted to applied science or technology. It is in the latter area that losses or abandonments of achievements are rare, for reasons that are obvious, in any applied or practical field. On the contrary, fundamental or wholly intellectual science, as well as philosophy, have in their whole history appeared intermittently and sporadically.

It is clear that Chinese, Indian, Greek, and Western philosophy differ recognizably in their presuppositions, in their problems, in their methods of approach. We might also justifiably speak of an Indian and a Greek and a modern Western style of mathematics. Ancient and recent astronomy again, or for that matter ancient and modern physics, differ in the same way. As for the fact that many new fields of science have been successfully developed only in the past two hundred years, this might legitimately be rephrased to say that in chemistry, in biology, in geology, the Greeks failed to develop a true style, whereas modern Westerns did develop such styles.

A next step might be to raise the question whether the concept of style can properly be extended still farther into entire civilizations or whole cultures. Can these be spoken of as differing in style? Obviously this would be possible without undue violence. The question is, is there profit in penetration of understanding through making this extension and viewing whole cultures as stylistic expressions?

It is clear that no human culture can be devoted entirely to creativity. There are many needs, physiological and economic, that must first be satisfied. There are also adjustments that must be effected in the social sphere. The constitution of the society which possesses a culture, as well as the environment in which it subsists, are bound to enter into the shaping of the entire culture, so that such total style as it achieves would be far from pure. In fact, the stylistic quality of any total culture might be so muddied as to be discernible with difficulty.

On the other hand the importance of creativity is so great in culture that it may be justified to inquire how far it is legitimate to define qualities of style in total cultures.

II. Thinking about Style

The mental processes called for in dealing with styles are somewhat different from those ordinarily used by the historian or scientist: they are discriminatory, but can scarcely be called outrightly analytical. Although differentiations are recognized in determining styles, analysis is mainly used after judgments have been made. The primary act of judgment in regard to style is one of recognition. It is analogous to the judgment we make when we identify an individual as being himself and not another, or when we identify an organism as belonging to this and not to that species. The beginner may do this by analytic comparison through step-by-step diagnostic differentiation. With experience, however, the judgment often is total, immediate, and final. It has some of the qualities of both an analytic and synthetic determination, but as a mental act it is neither synthetic nor analytic. Further, it can be called neither inductive nor deductive, since it is not reasoned. It is scarcely abstract, because the judgment is after all a particular one as to individual identity or as to place within a pattern.

The faculties involved in such judgments go pretty far back in our organic phylogeny. They are used in recognition of place and in recognition of individuals. They are even built-in instinctively in some species, as regards recognition of species that are dangerous; monkeys seem to fear snakes even without experience of them. I am of course not arguing that when we deal with style there is anything instinctive involved. As human beings, we have to *learn* all the styles we recognize and operate with, and it is as individuals that we have to do this learning. My point is merely that something similar to a faculty which we build up in ourselves through experience and learning, does occur as instinctive in some lower organisms. Even our non-instinctive faculty of learning to recognize or identify or correctly remember a particular place or person runs back pretty far in evolution.

The creative artist undoubtedly is highly sensitive in his ability to recognize both particular and patterned or stylistic identity in the field of his creativity. However, this faculty is one which is ordinarily not called for to any notable degree in the prosecution of scientific research, especially of the laboratory type. It does enter into many aspects of humanistic scholarship. In science it is perhaps most called for in the basic natural history aspects of biology—the accumulation of a broad organized body of underlying knowledge on which the remainder of biologic science largely rests, and which is often designated as systematic or taxonomic biology.

Aboard ship, David Starr Jordan was said upon occasion to run his eyes rapidly over a net load of fishes as they were poured onto the deck, and picking one from the miscellaneous array, to say, usually correctly, "Here is a new species." The new species would have been found also by less experienced ichthyologists, but only after much laborious comparison. Somewhat similarly, in the field of identifying painters of unascribed pictures, Bernard Berenson speaks of the convictions that sometimes arise out of nowhere, seemingly. He insists that these must not be disregarded, because in many cases confirmation follows when the necessary analyses and comparisons have been made.

When the subject matter is style, the approach is thus at the same time a style study both differentiating and holistic. It is also concrete. It may be reënforced by subsequent abstraction, but ordinarily it cannot begin with abstraction nor with reasoning. The concrete, qualitative phenomenon, or group of phenomena, is primary. The necessary first step is to associate a phenomenon with a pattern, and then in many cases to recognize its place within the pattern. The cardinal act might be said to consist in identifying the relation of phenomenon and pattern.

III. Synchronic Approaches

The intellectual apprehension of styles is normally diachronic, because styles occur in civilizations and civilizations occur in time and take time to build up. Beyond this, formulations may have a monistic or a pluralistic slant, according as they emphasize the continuity or the particularities of culture.

However, the approach may also be synchronic, treating a whole-culture as of a given moment, statically instead of historically. Formulations of the style of whole-cultures in this way have usually been done by anthropologists and for small cultures, whose history is little known or wholly unknown.

Formulations of this order have been made by Ruth Benedict and Margaret Mead, both of them anthropologists from Boas environment and Boas stimulation, which is now generally recognized as having been largely non-historic in its formulation of problems. Boas himself was permissive of their approach, but evidently only half approving of it. Wilhelm Milke in his three theoretical papers on ethnological method (Schmoller's *Jahrbuch*, 1937–1938), devotes one essay to this approach, which he frankly calls stylistic (Kultur Stile)—the two others being the atomic and historic method, and the functional one.

Both Benedict's and Mead's work of this type is avowedly holistic, directed at the totality of the culture dealt with. Both of them operate synchronically, or timelessly; and both emerge with psychologically slanted final formulations. Benedict was strongly impressed with the patterning of culture and she used the term "Patterns of Culture" as the title of the book in which she systematically portrayed and contrasted three non-literate cultures as total entities. However, the more she generalizes her patterns, the more do they convert into psychological concepts. I am not clear whether this is the inevitable result of trying to further and further generalize a group of co-occurring patterns. Certainly less and less of the constituents of the patterns is retained as this process of bringing a mass of them to a single focus proceeds. Perhaps a final, subsuming term or label *can* be only a psychological one. It may be that patterns of culture kept conceptually cultural will interrelate, but will not integrate in the sense of subsuming into a single general principle, and that if such is sought it must turn out either subculturally or superculturally psychological. Benedict's interest in culture patterns is evidently as a product. Her finishing designations are clearly meant as condensed descriptions of products, not as explanatory causes.

Margaret Mead's formulations avoid the label, or at least the single overriding label, and show more interest in formulating a dynamic pattern which is seen as shaping the personalities that express the culture. There is, accordingly, a partial endeavor in Mead's work toward the determination of psychological causation of cultural patterns.

Benedict made one effort to apply her point of view and method to a greater culture: in *The Chrysanthemum and the Sword*. Mead has delivered a good many opinions on American and other civilizations, but not systematically. Gorer's account of American national character is influenced by her, but she cannot be held responsible for it. In general these attempts to apply the synchronic holistic formulation to the larger civilizations have met with resistance and doubt. Certainly the great mass of anthropologists, both in Europe and America, have not attempted the method.

Kroeber's *Configurations of Culture Growth* differs from the work of Benedict and Mead in that it is diachronic and transcultural, and endeavors to be strictly inductive. This leads to most of the book being concerned with non-holistic activities of culture, such as painting or philosophy. The book barely reaches the level of civilizations-as-wholes in one chapter, whose misplaced title, "The Growth of Nations," has tended to obscure its subject matter.

A case can be made for Spengler's work containing, under its diachronic dress, a strong impulse to essentially static or synchronic formulation of each of the cultures he deals with. This point will be considered below.

IV. Diachronic Approaches—Monistic

We come now to consideration of diachronic attempts at apprehending civilizations. These may be divided into monistic and pluralistic approaches. This seems like a simple division of convenience, but it is more. The monistic approach tends also to be unilinear; its organization inclines toward separation of stages; and the idea of progress is usually prominent. Recognition of stages in turn tends toward systematization. Indeed it is evident that this line of thought is philosophical and that it emanates from philosophers or from those with a philosophic approach. Thinking along this line first took shape with Voltaire, unless one is ready to include Vico as a predecessor. It was Voltaire who coined the term "philosophy of history" and who first put the whole area of thought vividly before large numbers of people.

With his superb gift of narration, it is perhaps not surprising that a larger part of Voltaire's "philosophy of history" is actual history than it is philosophy. He did not use the noun "civilization" (though he did employ the corresponding verb and participle) but it is evident that he was *de facto* dealing largely with civilization as his fundamental concept. The title of his most systematic work varies, in its parts, its whole and its different editions, between *Philosophy of History* and *Essay on the Customs and Spirit of Nations*. With all his passion for enlightenment, Voltaire did not make a formal division of human history into successive steps or stages. This was first done by his successors. From our point of view Voltaire may perhaps be defined as a superb historian and man of letters who *en passant* reflected on enlightenment and unenlightenment and who engaged in some penetrating and cultivated but unsystematic philosophizing.

With Hegel and Comte we are definitely in the realm of outlines of universal history subsumed in three successive stages of progress. Of Hegel's posthumous work on the subject, first published in 1837, *Philosophy of History*, it is probably characteristic that the word "civilization" occurs in the book only once. Concern is with the much more transcendental entity "spirit" and its three stages of self-liberation. Hegel was capable of acute insights into the events of history, but he was not interested in developing them concretely except in the line of one idea. His inclination is away from particularizing about specific cultures or nations: he remains floating on a level above them.

Auguste Comte used to be hailed as the father of sociology, although modern sociologists have veered away from such ascription. He did coin the name sociology, and he envisaged a hierarchy of sciences with sociology as the capstone. His three progressive stages of human development are not concerned with liberty, as are Hegel's, but with methods of human thinking: the mythological, metaphysical, and positive-scientific. Beyond this simplistic tripartition, Comte's text is strewn perhaps more richly than Hegel's with specific historic judgments and insights; but these are only loosely woven into his systematic fabric.

Among our contemporaries, Northrop and Sorokin may be

mentioned as belonging to the monistic tradition. In both of them, acceptance and ultimate solution of the problems of civilization are achieved by balancing of antithetical factors. Northrop's duality is between an aesthetically immediate component and a theoretical one, in the civilizations respectively of the East and of the West. Disharmonies in civilization result from overbalance of one or the other factor, and harmony is to be effected by their reconciliation and integration.

Sorokin's dualism is not framed spatially but temporally. He sees a major cyclic swing of the pendulum between long-term ideational and sensate "supersystems," relieved only by occasional brief transitions of idealism or of breakdown. Sorokin's two phases are essentially descriptive, and he documents them with masses of chronologically dated cultural products. On the basis of his own voluminous substantiating evidence, his "ideational superphase," as it might well be called instead of his own "ideational supersystem," corresponds to the usually accepted formative or developmental stage of major civilizations, and his "sensate" to the fully matured and dissolving stage.

Sorokin is meticulous in distinguishing culture or civilization from society within the sociocultural realm, whenever the distinction is called for. On the other hand, he wholly denies integrational identity to cultures and civilizations, and looks upon them as mere spatial collocations or "congeries." He does grant integration, and therewith a degree of autonomy or identity, to what he calls "cultural systems," namely certain segments of cultures such as art, science, religion, and ethics. He also sees integration pervading his ideational and sensate supersystems which transcend cultures. This unusual position of Sorokin of denying integration to the usually accepted major entities of history, its "nations" or civilizations, while allowing integration to exist both in topical segments of civilizations and in certain qualitative and recurrent attitudes or outlooks that endure through and beyond civilizations—this anomalous position I can only see as somehow connected with Sorokin's propensity to erect a formal philosophic system. For instance, his 1947 book *Society, Culture, and Per-*

sonality: Their Structure and Dynamics is subtitled *A System of General Sociology*.

Northrop is a philosopher by profession who is strongly interested in cultures and their values.

V. Diachronic Approaches—Pluralistic

In a diachronic, pluralistic approach to the interpretation of civilizations, the philosophic cast or slant recedes, as is to be expected, before the empirical. The pluralistic construals are comparative; and may be described as attempts to work out a natural history of civilizations.

The line opens with Herder, a Baltic German born fifty years later than Voltaire, influenced by him, but of a fundamentally different temperament. Outside German literature as well as within it, Herder's influence has been most important as a critic and as a stimulator of folkloristic and non-classical interests. His propensity was for the remote and exotic and anonymous: he was an eighteenth-century romantic. His main work is called *Ideas on the Philosophy of the History of Mankind*. The derivation from Voltaire is obvious in the title; but the scope of the work is surprising. Only the second half of the book settles down to an actual tracing of the history of the known peoples of the world, with primary emphasis on their cultures. The story begins with East Asia, goes on to western Asia, to Greece, to Rome, to the marginal peoples of Europe, and so on, the last of its ten sections being concerned with Europe since the Crusades. The first half of the book is devoted to providing a genuine natural history, a history of our planet as the setting of human history. The first section is astronomical and geological. The next two are botanical and zoological. Then the structures, functions, organs, and energies of man are considered, followed by the varieties of his racial physiques and the environmental influences bearing on him. Then follows what might be fairly translated in modern terminology as a theory of human culture, which Herder variably calls "humanity" (*Humanität*), "tradition," or "culture" (*Cultur*).

This preliminary half of the book ends with a discussion of the origins of man in Asia. This sets man in his place in the world. Only then does the "philosophy" of his history of culture begin to be recounted.

This summary suffices to suggest a certain diffuseness, a quality with which Herder has often been charged. But it also indicates his interest in bases as well as in culminations, in nature as something larger that includes man, in multiple human efforts which, however, can also be viewed together as a totality of culture; and a recognition of all creative cultural products as possessing significance, equally so whether they have or have not led to our own modern civilization.

The Russian Nicolai Danilevsky made a more systematic attempt to treat the greater civilizations in the manner of natural history, being trained as a biologist, in botany and ichthyology. He was also a pan-Slavist, and motivated nationalistically to try to apply biological method to human history. His endeavor appeared in the book called *Russia and Europe,* first published in 1869 in a journal and two years later in book form. Danilevsky was evidently impressed by the transience of civilization, an old idea which underlies Gibbon's *Decline and Fall,* as well as numerous eighteenth- and nineteenth-century reflections on the succession and lack of duration of "nations" or "empires." As a pan-Slavist, Danilevsky was inspired by the evidences which he discerned of the decline and impending death of West European civilization, to which he saw as successor a Slavic civilization led by Russia. This is surely not a promising soil in which to expect the development of sound ideology accounting generically for civilizations in history; but Danilevsky's theory can readily be disentangled from his propagandist interests. He recognizes, besides an ethnographic pool of the pre-literate peoples, ten major civilizations in the Old World, plus two that perished in Mexico and Peru, with the Slavs as about to constitute the thirteenth. Each of these civilizations he attempts to construe as a "culture-historical type," a concept evidently based on the biological types of Cuvier. But, whereas the Cuvierian types are plans of fundamental biological organization, and are the pre-evolutionistic equivalent of phyla or grand lines of genetic descent containing innumerable variations, the culture-historical types of Danilevsky each consist of a single example only. Nevertheless Danilevsky's approach is commonsense and empirical. The result is that he sees his civilizations as separate entities, although running roughly parallel courses. In these two points he anticipated Spengler, and it is not wholly clear whether Spengler was influenced by Danilevsky directly or indirectly or not at all. Danilevsky is also somewhat simplistic in characterizing the growth and decay of civilizations as parallel to the growth and decay of individual plants or organisms. He evidently sees this resemblance as something to be taken for granted on the basis of the outward analogy. But at any rate he does not press beyond the analogy, nor endeavor to assign organic causes to the cultural growth and dissolution process.

With Spengler we encounter a very strong sense of style. He perceives the distinctive qualities of major civilizations with unusual sensitivity—sometimes even forcing imaginary distinctions. This is the easier for him because he recognizes only some six or eight civilizations. The pre-literate ones do not exist as cultures; the intermediate ones he disregards. He also cuts out from consideration what would ordinarily be construed as the later half or more of cultures, their period of maturity and decline. All this portion of their course he looks upon as merely fossilized non-creative culture, which he labels civilization, and refuses to deal with as being in "culture." Spengler's whole intellectual approach would have broken down if he had attempted to apply it to 21 or 29 separate cultures such as those of Toynbee. Throughout, he is given to simplifying situations and especially to exaggerating them.

In the same way he insists that his few genuine cultures are completely and totally integrated, without residuum. They each show a particular pervasive style in all their activities and products. If Spengler had limited himself to seeing some trend toward an integrated and coherent style in each civilization, many of us would be much readier to agree with him.

A corollary of the complete integration which he postulates is that separate cultures are impermeable toward one another. He makes an argument that they do not transfer content one from the other, or if they do, it is utterly changed, so that it can no longer be spoken of as the same content. This of course is simply contrary to the facts of all culture history, which, if it shows anything, demonstrates the tremendous amount of cultural content that has been not only transmitted by tradition internally within cultures but has spread cross-culturally.

A result of this gross exaggeration by Spengler is that his cultures become monads; they cannot take anything one from the other; they cannot influence one another; each runs its own course which is completely self-sufficient and unitary. They are something like Democritan atoms except that they perish of themselves, while new ones arise out of nothing.

It is in stylistic keeping with the picture that Spengler paints, that as his cultures are eternally separate and non-related, in other words wholly different but equivalent, so he also makes their courses uniform, both as regards birth and rise and fossilization as well as in actual duration. This duration he sets at 1,000 or 1,500 years, according as the prodromal nascent stage of each culture is excluded or included from the reckoning.

That the cultures must live a similar life and must die is a counterpart of Spengler's powerful sense of doom. It is an exaggeration as regards the facts of history, but it heightens the picture. In trying to set up a concept of fate as a substitute for the concept of cause, Spengler again exaggerates. It is true, in dealing only with the history of nations, that close agreement as to the causes of particular events is rare as between different historians. Causality in human history is so diverse in kind, and the causes are so many, that it is exceedingly difficult to agree upon their respective roles, or even to ascertain them all. In actual practice historians aim to select and portray what is "significant" rather than to give definite explanations of why things happened the precise way that they have happened. Of course this is increasingly true as larger and larger units of history are taken as the subject of inquiry, until we come to those greatest units which we call civilizations. Sorokin has pointed out how logico-meaningfulness is a quality better attained by historical research than are causal-functional relations. One may quarrel with his somewhat awkward terms, but there is little question that, especially in the realm of culture, the significance of historical phenomena can in general be ascertained more successfully than can their causes or functions.

The whole matter of doom, of course, is an unfortunate distraction because of its heavy emotional weighting. Danilevsky already predicted it, but as a Russian he was an optimist as to the future because Slavdom had not yet matured. Spengler came a half century later and as a German was a European, although a marginal one; and he used breakdown as an aesthetic device to heighten the picture he painted.

One final criticism that must be made of Spengler is that his study is not really comparative—at least it is not freely comparative. Essentially he has worked out with some elaboration a contrast between the Mediterranean classic civilization and the subsequent Occidental or European one. This viewpoint he admittedly took over largely from Nietzsche. Nietzsche however derives from Goethe, and most of his Apollinian—Dionysian contrast, which Spengler called Apollinian-Faustian, can be found set forth poetically and in full in the second act of the second part of Goethe's *Faust*—the Helena episode.

To this pair of cultures, which he knew well, Spengler added as a tertium quid of a fulcrum an imaginary civilization, the Magian one, overlapping the two preceding in time as well as in space, although apart from "basic symbols" he has relatively little to say about this third culture. As for China, India, Mesopotamia, and Egypt, Spengler is, when analyzed with care, incredibly meager in substantive content, in what he has actually to report about them. There are some brilliant flashes, but vast silences and darknesses between.

Toynbee is not only a trained historian but the only historian in the group of the pluralistic interpreters of civilizations under consideration. He has reacted with moderation and vast empirical knowledge to the dogmatism and exaggeration of Spengler. But he is also partly derived from Spengler, as shown by his near acceptance of Spengler's Magian culture, which he renames Syriac. He goes far beyond Spengler in refusing to simplify his task by dispensing with inconvenient cultures. His array of them is between 20 and 30, according as some of the more "arrested" or "abortive" ones are or are not included. He arranges all these according as they are derived or partly derived from one another, "affiliated" and "apparented"; and he does not hesitate to view two pulses of civilization in the same area as two separate civilizations—if they are not overwhelmingly repetitive.

Toynbee calls his units sometimes civilizations and sometimes societies. He is really thinking more often in terms of societies, that is, aggregations of men and their minorities and majorities, than he is thinking of cultures. Consequently questions of style hardly obtrude in his work. He does not deny style, but he does not seriously consider it as such. Also, dealing primarily with men or societies of men, or elite and proletarian groups within the societies, he is necessarily more concerned with events than with configurations of either culture or style. And this in turn brings it about that he deals far more with directly efficient causes that reside in men than with the meaningful patterns that culture assumes. The ultimately significant causality which he finds is that of the moral attitudes of men toward their societies, especially in the privileged minorities.

These are factors pretty far removed from considerations of how far a stylistic unity pervades a culture. The challenge, which when successfully met by society's elite, results in the genesis of a civilization, may be physical or social; if the latter, it is usually the disintegration of a previous society. After a period of prosperity and growth, Toynbee finds that certain events are likely to occur: a time of troubles, a universal state, a universal peace, and final breakdown. It is apparent that all these larger events or states are essentially political and moral. So again Toynbee does not really come to grips with culture; the question of how far this may represent a unified style scarcely arises in his mind.

On the other hand, Toynbee's repetitive sequences of events, his formula of expectable events *a, b, c, d,* disconcerts historians. It is perhaps this which has led to their general resistance to Toynbee's scheme: the opposition is on sound procedural grounds.

VI. Problems and Procedures

It remains to review the problems which confront the student of civilizations, the procedures which it is advisable to follow, and the assumptions that may or must or should not be made.

First of all, I think it may be agreed that successful insight into the nature and history of human civilizations or cultures will be made via an empirical route, by means of something akin to natural history.

If so, the first step after accumulation of data would be organization by means of classification—a classification of the facts as they come associated—in the world of nature, if one prefers the wider term, or in human history if one prefers the more limited.

Everyone would like even better than classified organization an understanding of the processes of sociocultural change and development. But we shall determine and understand the processes more soundly after our data are organized.

I believe that we shall have to deal with more than the 21 or 29 societies or civilizations of Toynbee. On the other hand, these will not be all on one level, but will undoubtedly organize into superordinate, coördinate, and subordinate ranks. Toynbee has himself made a notable beginning in this respect, but considerations of social magnitude, of cultural intensity, and of the stylistic qualities of cultural patterning will also have to be given weight in our ordering of the array of civilizations.

An assumption that will have to be accepted is that of the interconnectedness, in some degree, of *all* cultures. In particular cases the problem will be that of the degree and content of connection. The total amount of cultural diffusion that has taken place over this earth is enormous, but the quantities also vary greatly according to time and place.

Generic trend toward accumulation of culture content will have to be recognized for total human culture, and a tendency in the same direction within particular cultures. So far as this trend exists it will operate in the direction of uniformizing rather than differentiating, and therefore as an impediment to the recognition of cultural styles. The trend must however be accepted as a fact, irrespective of whether it makes difficulty or not. And the stylistically attuned will tend to see the secondary stylistic differentiation more readily, and with greater conviction, than the underlying connections.

That there is a trend toward progress will also have to be accepted. Such progress is manifest in the total quantity of culture controlled by societies, and making therefore for mastery of the environment; in the size of the cohesive social unit, internal and external; and in recognition of reality. Many anthropologists are still shy of admitting any sort of cultural progress; but this is an outdated position. In naïve days there was indeed much ethnocentric assumption of progress that was false; but these are no longer naïve days. We can fully accept cultural relativism, and yet not make of it a curtain that obliterates all deeper inquiry into values. The question is, what cultural progress we can actually determine with weighed evidence, after cultural relativism is accepted.

It is of course also to be assumed that cultural progress is not steady but more or less vacillating. There are setbacks and losses as well as gains, and these are important precisely in delimiting civilizations one from another.

Pulsating growth and atrophy are most readily traced in the

field of creativity and style. Creative products of culture are in some ways the best index of cultural growth, perhaps because they represent the products of leisure and reserves, the flowering of cultural growth.

The phenomena of style need handling, in investigation, somewhat different from many other cultural and historical phenomena; but they are not intrinsically more difficult to deal with. Style has indeed a subjective aspect, especially in connection with the emotion released as style is apperceived. Nevertheless the phenomena of all style also have an objective aspect. That they are often most readily identified by simple recognition does not mean that the recognition rests permanently on mysterious or rare subjective faculty: it rests also on experience with and exposure to the phenomena; and verification can always be expressed objectively.

When cultural growth is spoken of, or cultural growth and atrophy, decay, disintegration, and death, these are metaphorical terms used descriptively. The terms are analogical when applied to human culture, but their use of course does *not* imply that processes of biological growth and decay are being referred to or utilized. It can be assumed today that no scholar sophisticated enough to deal sensibly with cultural phenomena is really an organicist.

Every cultural growth involves first of all the acceptance, by traditional inheritance or by diffusion from elsewhere, of a body of cultural content; second, an adequate adjustment to problems of environment as well as social structuring; and third a release of so-called creative energies more or less subject to shaping by the factor of style. These three components co-occur and interinfluence one another. Ultimately they can produce a defined and unique whole-culture or civilization, which is also a nexus or system of style patterns.

In time the creative activities become somewhat like active growing points. They then do most to shape and color the style of the culture; but they are never overriding or wholly determinative of the civilization.

The fact that the style of the whole culture is always secondary and partial, of course does not deprive it of significance.

Both creative styles and whole-culture styles seem to grow and decay in irreversible courses, but can also reconstitute themselves. Attempts at reconstitution—widening of the base of the style—are fairly frequent and sometimes successful.

When reconstitutions fail in most segments of a culture at about the same time, and it breaks down and is largely superseded by a foreign or a new culture aggregate, we can legitimately speak of its termination or end—"death" in the popular parlance, for that particular cultural constellation.

Such endings are important in the classification or "periodization" of cultures. They are like a "dark age," after which slow accumulation and growth is gradually resumed.

Of course no dark age is ever a complete extermination. As already said, all cultures are interconnected, and those which succeed one another in more or less the same area inevitably maintain some continuities, even when much violence is imposed. Obviously too, reconstitutions accomplished in one or several segments of a culture, before the other segments break down, involve much less destruction and regression of total culture.

If reconstitution of some segments is accompanied by continuance of growth, or wholly new growth, in others, the reconstitution can be relatively painless and without constriction. Reference here is to the type of reconstitution which took place in "Late Mediaevalism" of the fourteenth and fifteenth centuries after the florescence of "High Mediaevalism" of the thirteenth century had ended, and before the Renaissance, which ushered in the modern pulse period of Western Civilization, had reached its culmination.

Note on Some Word Usages

The verb "civilize" and its participles go back, in French, to Montaigne and Descartes (Febvre) or to Bodin (Wundt); in English, to 1631–1641. The noun, *civilisation*, first occurs, according to Lucien Febvre, in Boulanger's posthumous *L'Antiquité Devoilée* of 1766. A 1752 occurrence attributed to Turgot is spurious, due to insertion by a reprinting editor. Voltaire, Rousseau, Turgot, Buffon do not yet use the noun, although d'Holbach and Diderot do in 1773 and 1774. *Civilization* appears in the Academy's dictionary of 1798. English usage lagged somewhat. Johnson excluded *civilization* from his 1773 dictionary in favor of *civility*; Ash in 1775 included it, and as denoting a condition as well as an act.

Volney, by 1814, already uses the noun in its broad or ethnographic sense: *la civilisation des sauvages*. Ballanche in 1819 seems to have been the first to use the noun in the plural, with comparative and relativistic implication.

The word passed into German, but remained secondary to *Cultur*, later *Kultur*. Kant uses *Civilisirung, civilisirtest*, but *Cultur* more often. Hegel seems to employ *Zivilisation* only once in his *Philosophy of History*. The term Culture History (*Geschichte der Cultur, Culturgeschichte*) dates from Adelung, 1782, and Hegewisch, 1788. The original meaning of *Cultur* was cultivation. The sense of the condition resulting from cultivation emerged later and gradually—as with *civilize, civilization* in French and English—and it is doubtful whether any German before about 1850 used *Cultur* strictly and exclusively in its modern scientific sense of culture as a product and a state rather than an action.

This scientific sense of *culture* was introduced into English by Tylor in 1871, basing on the German ethnographer Klemm, and was not recognized in English dictionaries until 1929–1933. The word had just been popularized in 1869, by Matthew Arnold, with its older normalizing sense of the "pursuit of perfection," which by then was receding in German.

Before 1871, Tylor himself used *civilization*. He evidently abandoned it for *culture* because the latter was the more general in applicability, carrying in English no implication of degree of development, as *civilization* had come to carry it.

French was very slow in admitting culture as a technical scientific term in the Tylorian sense, being preceded in the use of it by Spanish, Russian, and Scandinavian.

In Germany there were several attempts to enforce a distinction between culture and civilization. One group wanted to reserve civilization for the more spiritual aspects, another group for the material and technological components of culture; and to Spengler civilization was merely the final, sterile, uncreative stage with which cultures end. These conflicting efforts perhaps are echoes of the dichotomizing of "Geist" from nature which idealistic philosophy imposed on German thought.

Elsewhere, no serious need seems to have been felt to contrast civilization and culture, and the two terms have been used as near synonyms, or at any rate as overlapping more than differing. In any scientific or scholarly context, for instance, "uncivilized" would today be construed as a slip into popular, ethnocentric usage, to be read as "less civilized," not as an implication of complete lack of culture.

"Philosophy of history" meant to Voltaire, when he coined the phrase, what we would call "science of history" if we were naming it (or his intent) afresh. The phrase has a pleasant ring, which makes it attractive to belles lettrists and librarians, but corresponds to nothing actual in the organization of scholarship; much as "enlightenment" would not today denote any one specific current of thought or knowledge.

A fortiori with the term *Geist*—"spirit"—which German has had such difficulty shaking off. It is now a half century since Rickert showed that if *Geist* means anything in a scientific context it means culture. Hegel's *Philosophy of History*, an ambitious and able effort, has lost relevance to concepts rooted in nature, because it revolves on the pivot of transcendental "spirit."

Another term that is often loved for its emotional connotations is "fate," Spengler's *Schicksal*. Spengler's strong sense of pattern made him realize that causality is infinitely complicated in the larger cultural reaches of human history, and that much search for definite causes in this area has to date been illusory, whereas apprehension of pattern becomes progressively deeper.

But that cause is difficult to isolate in a field is no reason for denying that it is operative there, and least of all is it justification for substituting an anticausal concept like fate, which demands an exempted position within the realm of experienced nature. Fate is of course a tragic word, but mankind does not have to see its history as all tragic, as Spengler and Nietzsche liked to, anymore than to see it all comic, cynic, bitter, or elegiac. These are temperamental flavors which pervade, but we can hardly found an intellectual interpretation of the human career on a preference for a particular flavor.

"Doom" is obviously even more affect-laden than fate, and therewith less susceptible of clear apprehension of reality. Expressionistic Germans like the emotion-charged term, Anglo-Saxons mostly prefer it somewhat diluted. Spengler's *Untergang* applies to the sinking of a ship, the setting of the sun below the horizon—night is on. We translate with "Decline"—it is still afternoon, perhaps a gentle, sunny afternoon.

"Crisis" is another term in favor at the moment, especially on the west side of the Atlantic. It makes us feel that we and our days are important and momentous: a great struggle is on; but we can still assume there will be a happy outcome, while being titillated by seeming danger.

"Cycle" and "cyclic" are beginning to have vogue nearly equal with "crisis." They are perhaps less affective, but they are mostly quite indefinite in denotation and are used because they are liked as words. "Cycloid" has a definable mathematical sense, and the sunspot, lynx population, and business cycles relate to statistically significant near repetitions of indubitable and measurable phenomena. For the rest, cycle and cyclic can take on any of several meanings, and are thus loaded with confusion for some. They are presently best avoided altogether in the realm of the history of culture.

7. Holism and World View

I. Holism

ROBERT REDFIELD, examining national character studies, points out that (a) these are timeless cross-sections of historic nations or civilizations and (b) that they formulate uniques which are not generically definable or comparable. This must be admitted. Such studies are comparative-contrastive in purport. The similarities in national character lie in the genus "nation" or family "civilization"; or beyond that in "human nature." This uniqueness of national characters is similar to the uniqueness and particularity of the units of which national characters are the highest collective expressions, namely human individuals or personalities. These are "given" in nature to such an extent that they are primary facts of experience not in (operational) need of definition. Nations and civilizations are not so completely given as are human personalities (they intergrade somewhat at the edges), but mostly they are so obvious in their mass as to require only a secondary degree of definition by distinction.

Redfield, speaking of the "classical primitive isolate" of Meyer Fortes, points out that this is but the smallest and easiest exemplar of a culture series leading up to nations and civilizations, which all are *naturally holistic*. That is to say, each unit contributes a system which is internally intelligible (even though the total

---

Read before the Comparative Civilizations Symposium at the Center for Advanced Study in the Behavioral Sciences, Stanford, California, spring, 1958.

causality which has brought the unit into existence may be partly or largely external to it).

II. World View

The problem was pursued [in the symposium] by Ethel Albert, Charles Wagley, and Arthur Wright for particular civilizations (Urundi, Latin America, China), although the three authors used different terms: "World View" (Albert); "Ideal Patterns" (Wagley); "Self-Image" (Wright). Daryll Forde in his 1954 book calls them simply (African) "Worlds."

The "worlds" consist primarily of each society's own culture, so that "world view" and "self-image" are largely the same. This image is always idealized, so that "ideal pattern" is an equally justified term, differing only in stress.

This idealized collective self-view is imposed on the history, law, religion, and every other intellectual product of the culture. As Wright says, it distorts the facts and blocks the supernational historiographer. It is also inevitably the first picture received by an ethnologist inquiring into a culture. It has the merit of being an organized and coherent picture or story, and is therefore always of operational significance. Being an idealization, it must of course be transcended by the searcher for reality. At the same time it remains a component of the final picture or story. This is because the image, though a product of the culture, is also a feedback and influence upon it. In fact, it may be surmised that a society with but a feeble or blurred image of its culture would have difficulty in realizing and attaining a sharply defined or vigorous culture.

The world or social self-view is obviously a counterpart of the Freudian super-ego, the Jungian persona.

III. Creators of the Image

Wright pictured the Chinese self-image as shaped by the literate gentry—no doubt correctly. In India, it would have been the Brahmins; in Rome, the patricians. It is to be expected that the formulating class will always have: (a) considerable power; (b) articulateness, including primacy in writing within a literate culture, perhaps religious knowledge in a non-literate; (c) and to be motivated *both* by idealism and self-interest.

A degree of resistance from other classes is expectable, but there is probably always considerable acceptance by the mass of the society. The plebeians accepted and fought for the patrician image of Rome, while gradually demanding a larger participation in the fruits of its successes. It is conceivable that Roman civilization deteriorated and was superseded when the whole of Roman society had become culturally plebeianized and the Roman self-image was blurred and incoherent.

In Rome, Livy in history and Vergil in poetry were prominent in giving the world-view its definitive formulation. In Greece it would be Homer, Hesiod, Herodotus, Thucydides, and the philosophers. In Portugal, Camoens was probably the most important. In non-literate Urundi, we do not know.

For most non-literate cultures we shall expectably never know. Where there was sufficient economic margin, priests may at times have led the way, or Paul Radin's "primitive philosophers." There is generally less class differentiation in non-literate than in literate cultures, and the formulation may mostly have been more democratic—with the storytellers and others helping to define or clarify the image.

The self-image varies in definition and coherence. The Yurok and Mohave images (though quite different) are more precise than those of Pomo and Yokuts. The Navaho view is more elaborate than that of the Walapai, and the Zuni and Hopi more coherent than the Navaho.

In the narrow worlds of primitives, their own culture occupies most of their knowledge of and interest in the world, so that self-image and world view are largely coincident. The same is considerably true of the earlier literate cultures. In spite of much surviving ethnocentricity, the civilization originating in Europe seems to have been most successful in partly separating self-image and world view, through widening of the latter.

IV. Isolation

A factor to be investigated is how far a cultural self-image can be built up without contrast to other cultures. In considering this problem, self-image may have to be distinguished from world-view, and cases of complete isolation (Easter Island, Polar Eskimo) will then be of importance.

On the other hand, *relative isolation* may be an aid in the building-up of a sharp self-image: Egyptian, Chinese, Polynesian, even native Australian. This is in contrast with societies and cultures exposed to many and changing contacts with others.

If other cultures are swamped by Western civilization, which presently appears to be an impending, world-wide phenomenon, then protective isolations will be largely wiped out. It is possible that world views and self-images will then be contrastive by time periods rather than by areas of rooting and occupation.

PART TWO

The papers of Part Two have to do with the relations of anthropology to the sciences, exact, natural and social, and to the humanities. Kroeber is keeping history within view as closely in discussing these relations as when his attention is upon civilizations, although the angle of vision is quite different.

Perhaps something should be explicitly said of Kroeber's "sense of history." The papers here indicate that this sense was at least twofold: the stereoscopic vision by which events and elements in culture and whole cultures are seen in depth and flow through time; and the "operational" aspect of history—how it communicates, its canon and style. Communication in history, and in anthropology, says Kroeber, rests on lucid and exact and full presentation of the data—its concrete events and elements—and their binding into meaningful relations. The narration should be in the customary vocabulary and, so far as the writer is able, in the best literary tradition of the language and prose style to which historian, or anthropologist, belongs. Mathematical and statistical analysis and synthesis, maps, charts, linguistic, and other element lists however specialized, even the experimental paraphernalia of the psychologist, when it is pertinent, may supervene, so long as intelligibility is kept. No method *per se* is barred; but obscurantism, bad or pretentious writing, and the use of "cult" vocabulary are barred. This is the view which recurs in Part Two.

One further word, lest the title and the emphases of this book mislead some reader: Kroeber was of course totally aware that anthropology, as is history, is now commonly dubbed one of the social sciences. He referred to it as such himself when it was appropriate to do so; nor do I have any sense that he was too much troubled by what his subject was called or where administratively placed. That it should have standards of behavior and should remain itself was of the greatest importance to him.

"The Integration of the Knowledge of Man," which opens Part Two, was presented at Arden House in Harriman, New York, in October of 1954 to a group of scholars brought together to discuss the unity of knowledge, which discussion was one of a conference series initiated and conducted that year by Columbia University as part of the celebration of its bicentennial. It was printed in 1955, one of seventeen other papers by as many participants of the conference in a book entitled *The Unity of Knowledge*, and edited by Lewis Leary. The complete list of those taking part is included in the book. More than sixty in all—it is an interesting list, and some orientation as to its make-up is relevant to an understanding of the tone of Kroeber's paper. Pierre Teilhard de Chardin and Neils Bohr, Robert Lowell and Julian Huxley, Sir Richard Livingston and Theodosius Dobzhansky, to pick six of them, give an idea of their variety and quality. Kroeber's contribution was intended, as were those of the others, to open a door to fruitful discussion by way of each man's specialty. It was midway in the decade of the fifties, the period of Kroeber's thinking on culture history which it is the concern of this volume to explicate and follow a certain distance. To go all the way, the reader is on his own. This is because Kroeber was not a system maker; his generalizations came to him, and for the most part were recorded by him not only in the context of concrete, factual material, but actually imbedded in a matrix of some large body of facts.

The student of anthropology today may be unclear about Kroeber's implicit assumptions regarding his own subject and its relations to others. His statement at Arden House on integration of the various fields will—or should—convince the student that Kroeber placed himself and his subject among the humanities and in science—natural science.

The sense of the conference might be said to have been an effort at a high level of understanding to bring a twentieth-century kind of intercomprehension between the various sciences and humane studies, or between science as such and humane study as such: a modern equivalent to the old catholic scope of philosophy which concerned itself with all knowledge and all truth and hence used, as needed, the tools of science and mathematics, of documentation and aesthetics.

"What Ethnography Is," was written to preface a series of monograph articles on a variety of subjects and peoples under the general heading "Ethnographic Interpretations." It offers simple working definitions of ethnography, of culture, of history. But it is in fact a lively, somewhat didactic essay on ethnography's kin ties and friendships: with history and archaeology (close); with psychology, (respectful); with the social sciences as such (not good); with the Social Science Research Council (none). There are somewhat more extended discussions of ethnography's kin ties with linguistics and with the humanities, these being relations of intense concern to Kroeber throughout his professional life, but explicitly so during the 1950's.

In 1957, Kroeber attended the meetings of the Pacfic Coast Branch of the American Historical Society where he read paper 3, "An Anthropologist Looks at History." He was among old friends; there is a school of history on the West coast as old as its oldest colleges, which has always taken to the field to supplement written sources. Historians of the West, of Mexico, of Latin America and the Pacific, and ethnographers and archaeologists of the same regions are constantly coming on each other in the field or in the Huntington and Bancroft Libraries, or in the archives in Mexico City. And they use and understand each other's material. In this brief paper which gave us the book's title, the touch is light, indicating how essentially at home Kroeber felt with these historians. It ends on a note which psychologists, some of them, might ponder.

"History and Anthropology in the Study of Civilizations" is the last of the previously unpublished papers in this volume. It was presented at the Center's comparative civilizations symposium and is placed here in Part Two because of its "relational" emphasis. It demonstrates a "style" of presentation possible in the free-wheeling atmosphere of peers where a scholar may with impunity be both interpretive and imaginative.

At the spring meeting of the Kroeber Anthropological Society in

Berkeley in 1958, "The Personality of Anthropology" was Kroeber's amiable response to too many laborings of hypotheses, painfully set up, always proved.

The historiographer and scholar in whatever field, interested in a sophisticated, twentieth-century approach to the concept of progress will find "leads in" to ethnographic sources and "leads out" from such sources into the history of culture and the history of ideas, in "Evolution, History and Culture." The paper was first presented at the University of Chicago Centennial celebration of the publication of Charles Darwin's *The Origin of Species*, and first published in the series of volumes growing out of the extended symposium on Darwin which was part of the centennial program.

Perhaps the reader also will feel refreshed to find a discussion of Darwin and the importance of his work passing as it were through hospitably opened doors to the humanities.

The last paper in the book, "On Human Nature," follows the Darwin paper. It, too, recommends the pursuit of the truth about human nature by way of the well-known routes of data collection and history, organic and culture. But its tone is somewhat different from that of the preceding papers, and suggests what is the fact: Animal behavior and nature—human and non-human—fascinated Kroeber. They were forever causing him to pause, to turn from the heady contemplation of whole civilizations and millennia of time, to observe, record, and speculate upon the living, phenomenal world about him.

It might be an ant who foolishly tried to cross the smooth concave cone marking the lair of a doodle-bug (ant lion). Sitting Indian fashion Kroeber watched the ensuing battle to its prolonged but inevitable close, with doodle-bug digging his way backwards down into his lair, the still-struggling ant firmly clasped in his strong jaws.

Then there is the gray bat which has lived for many years in the shelter of the vines above our front door. Watching it led to many questions—too many unanswered, Kroeber complained—as to the sex life of bats and bat arrangements for feeding and care of the young, under the special conditions of hanging upside down.

When the Florida Marineland was something new under the sun, we made a detour of several hundred miles to spend days under that sun while Kroeber watched dolphins behave like dolphins. And I remember a day in Peru where he was doing an archaeological dig. We were at Ancon and Kroeber sat on a rock over the water from which he could see an octopus perhaps eighteen inches across, under another rock. They observed each other narrowly for hours, neither making a move unnoticed by the other.

"On Human Nature," recalls an unpublished paper of Kroeber's which was to have been the first chapter of another sort of history from those discussed in this book. The finished first chapter is on insectivores and is called, "Hard-bitten and Small."

But more interesting to Kroeber than insectivores, or even the benign and beautiful dolphins, were people, everywhere and always people and of infinite variety—*Man* the unpredictable, the *Animal* who somehow discovered or invented *Culture*, and thereby, the means to free himself partly if he so chooses, and who knows how far? from the whirling biological wheel.

8. Integration of the Knowledge of Man

IN THE EIGHTEENTH CENTURY there was no organized field of inquiry corresponding to anthropology. What Immanuel Kant dealt with under that name was a curious kind of psychology, perhaps most nearly a sort of preformation of social psychology. But the concept of cultural relativity was well established—though of course not under that term—in the minds of Voltaire and other members of the Enlightenment. There was also a fair-sized and accumulating body of ethnographic fact on primitive cultures, and some widespread knowledge and a wider interest in the advanced cultures of China, Egypt, and the antiquity of the Near East. Voltaire wrote the *Essai sur les Moeurs*, the first attempt at a total history of humanity, and he established the term philosophy of history.

Johann Gottfried von Herder, toward the end of the century, gave a remarkably broad base to his somewhat similar attempt. Only the latter part of his work is an actual history of humanity. The first half deals with the physical earth, next with the life upon it, then with man's origin, nature, structure, capacities, varieties, and environments—all considered generically—before the narrative proper begins. Recorded plus inferred human history is thus presented by Herder literally in the light of what was known

---

Reprinted by permission of the copyright owners, The Trustees of Columbia University, from *The Unity of Knowledge*, edited by Lewis Leary, Columbia University Bicentennial Conference Series (Garden City, New York, Doubleday & Company, Inc., 1955), pp. 125–149.

between 1784 and 1791 of man's place in nature. Herder became even more famous and influential as a critic, folklorist, and creative writer, so that as new knowledge overshadowed that which he had controlled, his four volumes of *Ideas* on universal history became outdated and largely forgotten. But after more than a century and a half they remain a sort of grandiose sketch of what anthropology still—or again—has as its program.

When in 1859 Charles Darwin's *The Origin of Species* suddenly transformed the point of view of the life sciences and earth sciences from a static to a dynamic basal assumption, this assumption was immediately extended from organic life to human culture. The idea of a progress of mankind had widely and fervently been believed for a century. But as a popular doctrine or hope or axiom this assumption of progress had had little confirmation from the fixed relations that mechanics and chemistry and physiology and comparative anatomy had properly enough prided themselves on discovering. Kant could go to science for an impressive understanding of the starry firmament, but when it came to men at the opposite pole he had still to turn his unaided sight inward to draw out, like a spider, the threads of the categorical imperative. With Darwin's long-overdue establishment of flow as a principle of the whole organic sector of science, a release was given to those eager to believe in progress, and they promptly extended evolution to specifically human development: to man's customs, and civilization. Therewith anthropology was launched as a directed, conscious field of study.

That the impulse came from Darwinian evolution is shown by dates. In the dozen years following 1859 all the older group of evolutionizing anthropologists published their main works: H. J. S. Maine, Johann Jakob Bachofen, J. F. McLennan, Edward B. Tylor, John Lubbock, L. H. Morgan; to be followed by A. W. Howitt, Andrew Lang, J. G. Frazer, E. A. Westermarck, L. T. Hobhouse on into the early twentieth century. In the same year as Darwin's *Descent of Man*—1871—there appeared Tylor's *Primitive Culture*, in which for the first time culture was explicitly named, defined, and dealt with as an operational concept of

INTEGRATION OF THE KNOWLEDGE OF MAN 103

science. Of this evolutionizing group perhaps the greatest number were jurists by profession; several were classical scholars, or philosophers; none were historians. One only had occupied himself with anything biological: Lubbock, and his preoccupation, significantly, had been with the social insects and their faculties.

The schemata this group propounded differed in detail and emphasis, and there were some debates among them. What they all had in common, however, was the belief that while human institutions tended to progress, the evolution was essentially natural, that is spontaneous, due to the character of the human mind. Arising from things immanent, the evolution was mainly in one direction or unilineal, and what were most significant in it were its uniformities. So far as differences were noteworthy, they were the differentiation of earlier from later stages of development. Other differences tended to be seen as accidentals of minor significance.

This was a set of findings unlike those of evolutionary biology, in which development was seen as divergent and multilineal, dissimilarities were as important as similarities, immanences were avoided as assumptions and resolved away as results (except for some claims for orthogenesis, and these were always resisted), and progress, while not denied in biology, became an incidental finding instead of the cardinal one.

There were several reasons for the difference between the courses of the biological and the anthropological evolution. The biologists were under relatively little temptation to yield to flattering self-centeredness in dilating on progress. They had ready, when they accepted the principle of evolution, an enormous body of unbiased knowledge of animals and plants systematically classified according to what was known of their total structures. This knowledge became immensely more significant under evolutionary beliefs, and its enlargement, correction, and refinement were stimulated thereby.

The extant body of knowledge of culture, however, had not been correspondingly classified by structural comparison. So far as it was classified, the classification was mainly by speculative assumption, and thus was not in position to be really enriched and deepened by acceptance of the principle of evolution. In fact, the study of culture still remains relatively retarded in analytic comparison.

For instance, zoologists have long recognized that the abnormalities of Australian mammalian fauna are due to an unusual degree of isolation of the continent, with consequent autonomous diversification on the specialized and rather slender marsupial base. It is now beginning to be clear that what is unusual in native Australian culture is the result of an analogous (though mainly much later) isolation. But until recently, it was more customary among us to try to identify the specializations of Australian culture with stages of universal culture—either speculatively logical ones or stages of European prehistory—than to inquire into the comparative nature of the specializations and from these to infer the presumable circumstances of isolation, contact, and development within the continent.

As the force of the first burst of evolutionistic interpretation of culture waned, several new procedures developed. One substituted diffusion by migration, trade, or contact—a historic process—for the spontaneous immanence of progress previously assumed. This took two chief forms: in England, a theory of primitive culture being highly static, of higher civilization originating once only in Egypt, of this being spread mainly by one other people, the Phoenicians, and of all subsequent higher civilization, whether in China, Europe, or Mexico, being derivative; in Germany and Austria, the assumption that there had been a half dozen original cultures, each autonomous, localized and highly differentiated, and that these had been carried around and mixed to form the known historic cultures of the world, whose original constituents could, with sufficient acumen, be analyzed out from the amalgam. The essential theoretical naïveté of these assumptions of an origin (and an unexplained one) or of a handful of such origins is patent; and the naïveté is without parallel in biology—at least no parallel is known to me. But introduction of the historic principle of diffusion of culture did indicate aban-

INTEGRATION OF THE KNOWLEDGE OF MAN 105

donment of the former reliance on verbal or mystic explanation by immanences.

About the same time, in fact a bit earlier, the figure of Franz Boas loomed up. Trained in mathematics, he began as a physicist, and physical and then human geography bridged him into cultural anthropology. Boas was unsympathetic to the assumption of progress, which he recognized as emotionally founded, and he was hardheaded enough to realize that the enormous variety shown by human culture was very unlikely to be accounted for by any simplistic assumptions of either spontaneities or a few specific diffusions. He was not terrified at admitting a complexity of factors, and he cheerfully pointed out their variability in particular situations. In the earlier part of his career he still spoke occasionally of searching for laws which determined culture; later, he was skeptical of them. With this critical, realistic attitude, and the great range of his inquiries into almost all facets of culture and language, it was no wonder that he arrived at no organized synthesis. Many who were impressed by the power of his intellect were nevertheless disappointed at his presenting them with no single theoretical system. There is nothing to show that Boas was a pluralist from choice, but the phenomena seemed to him to lead consistently to plural interpretations.

It would appear, from what is now nearly a century of experience, that close-up analysis of process in a wide range of cultural phenomena, not preslanted toward a directed outcome, will usually eventuate plurally and variable and seemingly low in coherence. In fact, precedent of the underlying organic and even inorganic sciences would point to such an expectation.

II

Frontal attack on organic phenomena as a whole, from the angle of explaining change and recognizing process or cause, did lead to a series of relatively unintegrated findings analogous to those which Boas bequeathed to anthropology a dozen years ago. Separate approaches had to be developed for various aspects of the phenomena. For instance, physiological processes were gradually discovered by controlled observation, test, and experiment directed at those phenomena which were internal to individual organisms. They then proved not only to interrelate among themselves but to be exemplifications of suborganic, mainly chemical processes. In short, they "reduced," at least partly, to chemistry.

At the same time, common-sense recognition of the diversity of kinds of animals and plants was deepened by analytic examination—largely *without* the artificial insulation of experiment—into scientific anatomy. And this analysis in turn was enriched by ever widening comparison into a classification of organisms which became successively a more natural one, that is, successively corrective and cognizant of more traits of more organisms in the totality of life. Finally, at the spark of the idea of natural selection, this static classification, as we have seen, exploded into the more significant evolutionary one.

And when a generation later Gregor Mendel's second spark touched off the new experimental science of genetics, a further dimension of understanding was added to the doctrine of evolution and to taxonomy. So we do now at last begin to know something, and some of that experimentally verifiable, of the processes by which the earth's plants and animals came to be as they are. But the understanding still all rests—intrinsically, as well as in the time order of its development—on the slowly and coöperatively worked-out classification of living and extinct forms. The hasty or shallow-minded tend superciliously to regard such classification as a mere lowly mass of itemized facts gathered by those not bright enough to theorize and then verify by experiment. They forget that there is no branch of science which does not live and depend absolutely on an organized body of basic factual observations.

There are other biological sciences—cytology and embryology, for instance; but there is no need to elaborate the point that an early simultaneous attack by them all in their still undifferentiated condition would have led only to spotty and incoherent results. Nature always presents a first aspect of a welter of crude phenomena. It is the provisional isolating of particular facets or aspects in this chaos that makes possible the organization of corpuses of fact, then leads to integration with related corpuses, and finally to association with founded and definable processes—instead of illusory, verbal, speculative, or unverifiable processes.

III

The notoriously late development of chemistry in the history of Western sciences also carries a precedent for the sciences of man. The chemical aspects of most natural objects are complex, as compared with the mechanics of our limbs, of the age-old simple tools which are extensions of our limbs, and of the sort of solids and liquids we handle in everyday life. A genuine physics of masses and their mechanics therefore got established in Greek days; but the foundation of genuine—that is, permanent—chemistry occurred only in the eighteenth century. The basic chemical problem had long been correctly intuited to be an association of the varied qualities of the substances of nature with primal elements. But where progress bogged down was in the fact that vulgar thinking had provided four ready-made pseudo-elements —earth, water, air, and fire—which were really concrete exemplifications of the physical states of solid, liquid, gas, plus a sort of supergaseous. Yet, by reduction to these four elements, nothing consistently qualitative was specifically explained. Why they were of no help is clear when we realize that these elements are, in order, a variable mixture of compounds, a simple compound, a stably recurrent mixture, and a state of high molecular agitation.

The Hindus, characteristically subtilizing, added ether as a fifth and most rarefied element; the Chinese split earth into metal and wood, when they guess-philosophized materialistically. The Western Renaissance made a new, if fitful, attempt with three elements: sulphur, mercury, and salt—which at least was a warmer hunch than any before, with two of its three being true elements and the third a binary compound.

The next step was to become reconciled to the elements being numerous instead of only three or four, and to the fact that most of them were likely not to be included in the immediate experiences and sensory discriminations of our daily lives. Finally, with the postulates that elements were interirreducible, constant and measurable in their properties, and combinable only in definite multiple proportions, the gates of chemical progress were thrown wide. Yet the postulates that characterized the successful revolution were rendered possible only by possession of a body of genuinely chemical and reverifiable facts, mostly seeming random and unconnected while they were few, but increasingly coherent as they accumulated.

We are still groping in the sciences of man for our elements— in fact groping for definition of what properties shall characterize our elements so we may successfully determine them.

After nineteenth-century chemistry had discovered most of its elements, it began to realize that these fell into a system—the so-called periodic law—which enabled a successful approximate prediction of undiscovered elements occupying the vacancies in the system. When these vacancies were nearly filled there was the further and disconcerting discovery that transformations disturbed the hitherto assumed eternal permanence of the elements. Then knowledge began to accumulate on subatomic structure, which had previously been barred by definition. The result was that the elements of Lavoisier and nineteenth-century chemistry have now become elements only at second or third remove. What is significant in regard to this revolution of thought, however, is that the old elements do retain their validity and utility. It is simply that the frontier of interpretation has grown out beyond them: they are no longer the ultimates they once seemed. They are still operated with because they represent a sound distillation from out a vast body of verified knowledge. In fact, in one sense the old elements now represent a deeper understanding than they conveyed before the development of subatomic science—much as classificatory biology was not eliminated or dispensed with by the acceptance of the postulate of evolution, but was given greater accuracy and significance.

Well, to return to anthropology and the sciences of man, these seem to be in much the condition of biology and of chemistry at about the year 1700: they are making a valiant but diffuse total-front attack. This attack is too largely ineffectual because conducted without insight of the strategically vulnerable points; and that insight is lacking, or limited, because of the inadequacy of *organization* of a fund of controlled knowledge which is prerequisite. Thus, for example, we have not assembled in anthropology a digested classification of the cultures of the world, comparable to the natural classification of animals and plants that grew out of the Linnaean system.

As for Boas, perhaps it was because he came out of physics that he was impatient of classification and turned to process; but he also realized the difficulty of bringing experiment to bear significantly on cultural material. Similarly, although (or because) a statistician himself, he refused seriously to apply any quantitative approach in ethnology because of the inexactness of measurement of cultural phenomena. Further, perhaps also because he began as a physicist, he rarely developed historical problems of temporal sequence. He did respect historic context in comparison, much as a sound systematist respects total organic context—a thing which the early anthropologists had not always seen the necessity of doing. He brought in the specific past where he saw its bearing on specific present problems; but he remained without much impulse to infer or reconstruct the larger past of culture or to utilize the findings of prehistoric archaeology because he was absorbed in problems of process near at hand. This he could do because the scattering fragmentariness of results by such an approach did not disconcert him in his antisimplistic pluralism. But many of those who came after him were less tough-minded and sought relief in seemingly positive findings by new approaches, such for instance as the field of culture and personality. This field is certainly a legitimate area of inquiry, but one in which there exists as yet only a very insufficient body of organized knowledge on which to base conclusions.

IV

When we now proceed to consider systematically the sciences of man as a whole or of human behavior as they are sometimes called there would appear to be two considerations that cannot be omitted: first, the historical approach and, second, the concept of culture; besides which some reflections are in order on the interrelations of the several sciences concerned with man. While the writing of histories of experienced or documented human events of a public or political character is one of the oldest of organized intellectual activities, nevertheless what may be called the historical or sequential approach seems, on the contrary, to be late in science as a whole.

While history in its popular and most specific sense consists mostly of narrative, this is at times suspended to allow of description of a new people, of a city, of a condition or period. The difference between diachronic and synchronic presentation can therefore hardly be cardinal. We have descriptions included in histories, and narratives in works of geography, travel, and ethnography, ever since the times of Herodotus and the ancient official historians of China. In the wider sense, the narrative and descriptive sciences are alike in presenting facts in coherence—of time, space, or apparent cause. The phenomena are given as directly as possible and in their contextual relation of occurrence. This context is preserved: if explanations are made, they are marginal, as it were, and do not fundamentally disturb the context. This is the method of what in the earth and life sciences is widely known as natural history. The use of this very term natural *history* for a branch of knowledge that deals with phenomena far more by description than by narration is indication that the difference between these two techniques of narration and description is incidental to the more fundamental quality of organized presentation of knowledge with all possible preservation of the

INTEGRATION OF THE KNOWLEDGE OF MAN

data as such, in themselves and in their relations of occurrence. In short, it is a phenomenal presentation.

Such a presentation frequently contains an aesthetic as well as an intellectual component, and its interest may be in part aesthetically motivated or grounded. It does not, of course, *per se* constitute art because the aim is the intellectual one of knowing what actually is, of portraying reality, whereas art manipulates reality in order to imagine what might be or to express what is satisfying. However, that the aesthetic ingredient can be present in history and natural history is shown by the fact that the quality of their presentation is customarily evaluated in part by their literary quality and that authors like Herodotus, Pliny, Buffon, Gibbon, Humboldt are universally admitted into histories of literature.

This transitionality suggests that history and natural history belong at least in part to the undifferentiated matrix from which the more highly developed sciences and the full arts have sprung. They definitely cling to phenomenality. Contrariwise, the most scientifically developed among the sciences, such as physics which is usually the one held up as a model, dissolve away the appearance of phenomena, explain them by resolving them into something else: sounds into wave vibrations, for instance; differences of color into differences of wave length. By this resolution, a more penetrating understanding is attained, more generalization is achieved—causes and laws are discovered, in a phraseology which I try to avoid because many scientists have come to squirm at its application.

The immediately phenomenal and the metaphenomenal approaches occur side by side and supplement each other throughout science. They might also be called phenomena-bound and phenomena-resolving or simply phenomenal and theoretical, the latter resolving the context of actuality into one of less sensory and more general, abstract, and theoretical relations. This latter result is generally considered to be the aim and end of science, but it is obviously made possible only by the preëxistence of a controlled and organized body of phenomenal knowledge. This holds true on the basis of the axiomatic interdependence of percept and concept in the achievement of natural science.

Also there is of course no actual dichotomy of approaches but rather a polarity along an axis. Experimentation is a method of using artifice to remove a situation from its context of actuality into a context of theoretical relevance, focused on some critical point. Normally, experiment therefore belongs to the upper and later levels of the sciences. It may occasionally be applicable in simple form on the phenomenal level; but on the whole this level is characterized by observation. On the other hand, renewed observation of the actuality of nature is sometimes necessitated when theory and experiment have made clear the incompleteness of the observed record or have suggested its inadequacy.

Quantification also tends to become more important as a science proceeds from its phenomenal to its metaphenomenal phase. Like experiment it is fruitful in proportion as its relevance becomes apparent. Random measurement, like random experiment, would be even more stultifying than wholly random observation.

Even mere undirected common-experience observation has phenomena fall into patterns—the repetitions of celestial phenomena; the near-identity of individuals within species; the obvious, larger groups of families of terrestrial, plant, and animal forms which already find expression in prescientific language and thus provide a basis for the beginning of systematized or scientific classification. With the development of a science, its initial patternings are corrected and refined and ultimately resolved into explanations; but the patterns tend to be transcended or enriched rather than discarded.

V

Now as between the grand classes or segments of natural phenomena, it is evident that the inorganic ones yield most readily to experiment, significant measurement, explanation in terms of generalities, and successful prediction, and those of human behavior least so, with organic phenomena in the middle. The total of definite results obtained by the various sciences leaves no doubt of this being so.

Allied is another fact: namely, that as departments of science progress sufficiently and begin to establish interconnections, these connections assume a hierarchical form of steps, layers, or levels, the phenomena or certain aspects of them reducing or resolving from one level to another in one direction only: from the behavioral to the organic, from the organic to the inorganic. Behavior rests upon physiology, physiology is explained through biochemistry into chemical activities. Or again, culture (as a natural phenomenon) has society as a precondition; society, the individual; and the living individual again is first of all an organism.

These statements do not imply any crude materialistic monism; for it is not claimed that all the phenomena of one level are resolvable into processes of the subjacent level. In every case to date it has been found that the more basal processes will not explain all the phenomena above them. The features or qualities most characteristic of each stratum are fully intelligible only in terms of that stratum; in terms of its characteristic forces or at least its patterns. To assume nonresidual resolution of phenomena into factors of a lower level is generally construed as hasty or forced; and such reductionism has become an epithet of opprobrium in science.

VI

So far, the narrative and the descriptive presentation of data have been treated as complementary methods of the phenomenal stage of science, the employment of one or the other being according to situation and circumstance rather than expressive of any cardinal principle. It is now necessary to consider what is generally called the historical approach in the larger sense, leading to sciences that are historical in their nature and result, without their raw phenomena coming ready made in temporal order like the data of ordinary human history.

Astronomy and geology are considered historical sciences, and so are evolutionary biology and palaeontology. The sequence and trend of events constitute an integral part of their findings. On the contrary, the findings of physics and physiology are timeless—their processes are eternal or continuously repetitive. Time, in the form of its rate or speed, often is one of the factors that has to be taken account of in physics; but an over-all arrangement of events in absolute time is not one of the aims of physics or of chemistry or of physiology.

Yet the historical slant of modern astronomy, geology, and biology has not always characterized them. This slant is a recent development, scarcely appearing in astronomy before the eighteenth century, and not before the nineteenth in the others. If there was anything remarkable about the heavenly bodies to the Greeks, to the Middle Ages, and the Renaissance, it was precisely their changeless regularities. Our universe, this earth, the forms of life on it, were assumed to be fixed. It is not yet a hundred years since *The Origin of Species* spearheaded the break through the crust of this old postulate.

Perhaps the word historical is unfortunate in this scientific connection, because the unqualified word history first of all designates the narration of the doings of men and their societies, in which change, the unusual and extraordinary, the dramatic and accidental, are the subject, and the customary and repetitive are taken for granted or ignored. Human history is notorious for generalizing the least among all branches of intellectual inquiry; but astronomy, geology, and evolutionary biology most certainly aim at generalization and process. However, there seems no other available word, and historical will have to serve, at least provisionally, to indicate the tendency of modern science to discover developmental problems and aims that parallel in some measure the aims of historians of peoples and periods.

In the field of man, the core social sciences of economics, politics, and sociology have in the main been analytic rather than historical in their approach, but humanistic studies of languages, literatures, and arts are overwhelmingly historical—besides, of course, formal or outright history. However, it is notable that this tendency in the humanities is stronger in the present cen-

INTEGRATION OF THE KNOWLEDGE OF MAN 115

tury than in the last, and that it can hardly be traced back farther than the eighteenth century. Before that, humanistic studies inclined to assume a fixed standard form or norm, and to work toward this or to justify it, whether in inquiry into the arts or in languages. Contrariwise the historical approach is comparative, fluid, and relativistic even in its simplest form of passing from one period of an art, a language, or a national existence to another. And it is *a fortiori* when different though related or connected arts, languages, cultures, or nations are the subject of treatment. Significant in this connection is the fact that comparative philology, that is, the history of the Indo-European family of languages, began in the late eighteenth century from the realization that Sanskrit and Avestan were definitely similar to the idioms of Europe. It may be added that economic, social, cultural, and comparative history are all, essentially, developments of the past two hundred years.

We must therefore conclude that except for simple, direct recording and narration of public affairs and events, the historical approach is a late development in almost all intellectual inquiry. Most sciences begin by assuming an essentially fixed universe and expecting to discover the principles, laws, causes, forces, or regularities of their part of this universe. Apparently there is something in most human beings, or at any rate in most civilizations, that makes such discovery seem a desirable end, as well as one not too remote or difficult to attain. A recognition of unlimited flow, with endless intermingling of variable factors, with predictability at a minimum, and even change not certain, seems undesirable to most minds. It is discomforting at first acquaintance, and requires if not tough-mindedness at least a degree of sophistication to accept.

It is true that the inorganic sciences of mechanistic physics and static astronomy were the first sciences to undergo a reasonably firm degree of development, and also that narrative presentation of the doings of men and nations is the first example—and an example nearly contemporary with the beginnings of physics and astronomy—of use of the historical approach in intellectual activities. This coincidence has led to the view that an historic and therefore phenomenal approach is characteristic of the sciences of man or is more readily successful there, but that resolution of phenomena into processes is more characteristic and successful in the inorganic field, with the organic sciences falling midway. I formerly accepted this view of an inherent property of subject matter, and still hold to it in some degree; but its influence seems rather swamped by the obviously tremendous increase of historical interest, attitude, and approach in recent Occidental civilization. Nor is there any visible indication that this increase is merely a passing incident perhaps already over its peak. Rather does it seem that the tide of historicism is still rising.

Of course the growth of a sense of problems concerning the history of nature may not be construed to mean that the process sciences are receding or have shot their bolt. Physics and chemistry continue to flourish alongside astronomy and geology, physiology alongside evolution; and if on the level of human behavior no process sciences have so far emerged with any very firm foundation or great results, that is presumably a matter of "not yet" rather than of "no longer" or "receding."

It may be that the increase of interest in the historic aspect of phenomena is inversely correlated with impulse to ascertain origin —*the* origin of a phenomenon—in the comforting assumption that if the origin can be discovered the phenomenon will be explained. This is a naïveté of thought that is certainly less commonly committed than it used to be, and reënforces the suggestion that in general the historic approach presupposes a degree of sophistication.

VII

Man as a subject of science can be considered from at least three approaches: as an individual, as a social animal, and as expressed in his culture. The human individual is examined biologically in anatomy, physiology, and the other medical sciences, and as regards certain aspects of his behavior in psychology. Human

INTEGRATION OF THE KNOWLEDGE OF MAN 117

groups and societies are studied by physical anthropologists, by geneticists, in the social aspects of medicine, by social pychologists, by sociologists, and in some degree though not exclusively in economics, politics, anthropology. Human culture is the primary subject matter of the humanities as they deal with language, literature, art, religion; of the history of philosophy; of much of anthropology; of economics and politics; of jurisprudence and history, so far as these deal with the patterns and principles of institutions.

History as practiced by historians is the most difficult to classify. It deals, in complete mixture, with the fortunes and events of individuals and of groups, along with often some considerable dash of their customs, manners, institutions, and so-called cultural activities. It is regarded as the mother or at least the root stock of the social sciences. But it is easy to see why these social sciences have detached themselves: history seems to define itself essentially less by field or subject matter than by the channel through which it pipes its data: documentary record. Consequently, it knows no underlay or foundation beyond commonsense knowledge of human nature. To exchange or supplement this by an acquaintance with scientific psychology would seem abhorrent to most historians, and would probably be ridiculous in actual practice. History is the one field of professional study that knows no professional or technical vocabulary; and the only one that, though it interprets its data, attempts no generalizations, no theory that would tie it up with other intellectual activities. History is a self-sufficient end in itself: it is indeed scarcely a discipline.

These statements apply to the narrative history of events attributed to identified persons. Beyond this, its most elementary and perennial form, lie institutional, social, and cultural history, in which personal actors increasingly recede or even disappear, and the data have become generalized events or patterns instead of particular events. All the data of preinscriptional archaeology are of this order, most of past documented ethnology, much of the economic knowledge of former periods. Such facts and findings are in the social and cultural dimension; also they are anthropological, economic, as well as historical. Further, they permit and invite comparative treatment as the more random individual acts of individual men cannot be fruitfully compared.

However, comparison is one thing that historians boggle at—and with a sound instinct, granted their addiction to concrete particulars, since ultimate particulars are always distinct and it is the distinctiveness and uniqueness of events that are the true historian's preoccupation. The commonalities of common human nature as it is known to common sense are what the historian takes for granted to build on. So he claims as his such documented facts as illustrate the particular systems of trade, tillage, or taxation, systems of marriage, inheritance, or etiquette, the specific orders of architecture or styles of art, literature, or costume—in the nation, area, or period he is delineating. But when it comes to comparing systematically such phenomena as between India, China, and ourselves, or even between Christianity and Islam, or Greek civilization and our own, the historian gracefully retires in favor of the economist, anthropologist, or student of the arts. Astonishingly little culture history has been done by professional historians—less than by geographers (Friedrich Ratzel, Herbert J. Fleure), anthropologists (Berthold Laufer, V. G. Childe), economists (Max Weber), or by Sinologists and others (T. F. Carter on the history of printing, for instance) whose primary concern was with a civilization rather than the events of a region or period. And as for those who would compare the outline events of civilizations, the contours of the greater historic societies—the polite edging away from Arnold Toynbee is indicative of the sentiments of most historians.

VIII

At the opposite extreme from history is psychology, in that it does seek law or generalization; though it is still concerned primarily with individual men. I have just touched on the putative reaction of historians to a suggestion that they found their work on an acquaintance with formal psychology. The counterpart is the remoteness of many modern psychologists from sensing meaning in history; so far as I am in error, I shall welcome the exceptions with honor—subsequent to Gabriel Tarde, who was also a jurist, and Wilhelm Wundt, who was also a philosopher and ethnologist.

In fact, psychologists seem apathetic to the historical approach even in the broad sense and in fields related to their primary one of man. Organic evolution obviously deals not only with structure and form, but with function and behavior. Yet, in general, psychologists leave this rich comparative subject to biologists, though it is patent that the comparand of the ultimate basis of our human behavior must be found in subhuman behavior. True, there is the recognized field of animal psychology; but it is largely restricted to few species, and domesticated ones at that (from motives of convenience), and the findings are primarily of human pertinence rather than of total-organic comparative relevance.

The very lateness of recognition of psychology as an autonomous science is notorious. In China, in India, in Greece, in the Middle Ages, in modern Europe, it was always an appanage of philosophy; and at the same time it remained also the common property of the man on the street, including poets and historians as well as salesmen and adventurers. In my undergraduate days in the middle 1890's experimental psychology had just been recognized as a field by Columbia University and installed in an attic above the president and bursar on Forty-ninth Street. James McKeen Cattell, surrounded by instruments brought over from Wundt, lectured there to a class consisting of a woman (women were then very rare as students), a Japanese (equally rare), and Kroeber (soon to leave comparative literature for anthropology). In the belated peripheries at Berkeley in California, psychology remained within the Department of Philosophy until after World War I.

With the achievement of its independence, psychology set out to be a natural science, and was so accepted by the American

Association for the Advancement of Science and by the National Academy of Sciences. It made the mistake, however, in my opinion, of too largely choosing physics as a model and of emphasizing experiment as its method before it had determined the vital points in its soluble problems. So far as the model was not physics but physiology, there was no difference in principle—plus the added danger of reducing psychological results away as fast as they were got. The golden opportunity of basing on the behavior of whole living animals in a state of nature, first by observation, then by controlled observation, and finally by experiment at critical points—this opportunity was largely overlooked, because natural history and humble observation were unfashionable at the time, in favor of the magic fetish of laboratory experiment and test that had done wonders with inorganic material. Unfortunately, the material of human behavior—or mind, as it was then still called—is fairly refractory under the direct frontal attack of experiment. The results have thus been not indeed sterile—in fact for practical purposes the tests evolved have proved highly useful —but somewhat disappointingly meager as regards wider theoretical significance. The total-organism comparative approach would perhaps not only have yielded fresher and more stimulative findings to psychologists but might have invigorated biologists, for most of whom free-ranging behavior is a rather marginal field in which they feel diffident. It is a pity that so many psychologists have manifested a similar diffidence.

The most fertile imagination and original intellect in psychology to date, I understand Gardner Murphy to say, are Sigmund Freud's; and I fully concur—as I concur also in his opinion of the fertility and importance of Francis Galton. But I would add a *ceterum censeo:* Freud was preëminently imaginative and original through observation—not through experiment. That much of what he construed cannot be either proved or disproved is the fault not of his observing but of his possessing an unbridled imagination. Where he clinically observed longest and most closely, as on symbols, repression, regression, his concepts are presumably at least operationally sound, since they have been adapted and are used quite generally by psychologists. Where in the nature of things observation was least feasible and he relied on his speculative imagination, as in metapsychology and on the origin of culture, he has won less permanent following except among the elect.

Psychology seems in its whole constitution to be directed at man as an individual. Man in the abstract, in general, man as a species, if one will; but man understood through the individual, as in biology. But we have now with us the subfield of social psychology; and, more important, a strong tendency to classify psychology among the social as well as the natural sciences—as manifest for instance in university organization and in the research councils. I am not clear whether this drift to see psychology as a social science originated among psychologists and then was accepted by others, or the reverse; but I suspect the reverse to be largely true. Nor is the cause of the innovation clear. Was it due to a realization of the relative dearth of results by experiment, and a hope that the mass questionnaire might be more successful? I would rather suspect that the reason is the practical success of psychological testing in applied situations; and social science moving in an aura of practical utility or soon-to-be-attained applications, the bridge thus discovered came to be used.

This subfield of social psychology, by the way, was developed, in its American form at least, about equally by sociologists and psychologists, and sociology has never formally re-ceded it, which supports my guess that it was the applied aspects that moved psychology as a whole into the social sciences.

As for recognition of the dimensions of culture, it would seem that the central concern of psychology must be with the subcultural, the pan-human near-fixities, the universals of human nature, which have to be got at not from historically variable groups of men but as properties of the abstractable underlying human being dealt with as a concrete individual or a statistical average of individuals. Only, there is interposed between this goal and observable actual men a series of cultural veils that must be penetrated or allowed for, and modern psychologists are well aware of this fact. Culture, accordingly, exists for them chiefly as something that is an interference to be discounted or got rid of. It is rather in anthropology, where culture is a central theme, that the field of culture-and-personality relation has often been hailed as an approach that would deepen understanding of culture, or explain it—or to some make it more palatable.

IX

As for the social and cultural dimensions, it is sometimes useful to distinguish them, sometimes not. There are problems of pure culture, borderline ones, and again problems of social relations that are clearest when their cultural concomitants are subtracted. In all human matters the two dimensions coëxist. Anything cultural always applies to a specific society; no human society exists without an accompanying culture. It is therefore a question of operational profit, to be judged by results in each situation, whether to dissociate or leave associated the social and cultural aspects involved.

It is now a truism that the two aspects or dimensions are distinguishable in principle because societies occur among many subhuman species of animals unaccompanied by any tangible culture: it is only among men that societies and cultures are regularly coterminous. Animal associations range from the very loosest or transient aggregations to highly developed true societies more intensive than human ones, in that the survival of the species may be dependent on the success of the social functioning. Moreover, those intensively socialized species do not show more approaches to culture or foreshadowings or rudiments of it than do lightly socialized or unsocialized species.

In man, the social dimension relates not only to the group viewed as a group, as an entity. Features or properties characteristic of a whole group are on the average perhaps more likely to be cultural than specifically social. That the religion of Arabia is Islamic and not Christian or Buddhist or pagan is, strictly speaking, a cultural fact; for Islam and Christianity as such are, of course, both of them cultural forms, though as they both also serve certain social functions, their cultural nature may be overlooked or suppressed in favor of their societal aspects.

On the whole, as the sciences aiming at strictly societal findings have developed, they have tended to be less concerned with groups as entities and increasingly more concerned with the interrelations of individuals within groups—with intragroup relations. Sociology, for instance, has sought more and more contact with actual psychology, instead of assuming that it was dealing with collections of generalized abstract men. Here is the cause of the active participation of sociologists in the formulation of the field of social psychology.

Social anthropology as it is recognized in Britain is perhaps as fully concerned with interrelations of people in a culture as with the culture. The more specialized American social anthropology and much of the culture-and-personality study in America are even more weighted in favor of personal interrelations. Where interest is focused on social mobility, for instance, or on frustrations, culture really enters chiefly so far as its expressions or symbols are weapons with which people fight in their struggles with one another. In problems of the type of who-gets-what-from-whom-and-how, the who, whom, and how refer to interpersonal relations; only the what is partly or wholly cultural.

Broadly, sociology, as might be expected, has centered on social aspects, anthropology on cultural ones. But there is a good deal of overlap. For instance, P. A. Sorokin's most distinctive contribution about the ideational-sensate rhythm, relates definitely to culture. This is because Sorokin, being interested in grand contours and large systems, is driven to a telescopic use of history, and in this the interindividual struggles and adaptations are no longer visible. On the contrary, the anthropologist Homer G. Barnett in his recent book, *Innovation*, conducts a microscopic examination of how cultural changes begin and are carried on: what A's individual circumstances and motives are that make him turn his back on a suggested novel behavior, whereas B embraces it eagerly, and C merely drifts. In the focus of such dissections, psychological, social, and cultural considerations interlace. It is no wonder, accordingly, that Barnett sees little sense in the distinction of social and cultural factors: under his highpower lens his field is indeed a unit.

There are other features that distinguish sociology and anthropology, in spite of the fact that each must be sufficiently concerned with the other's subject of specialty to make the formulated theories of both activities almost identical. Perhaps the distinction is really between sociologists and anthropologists—their differentiation in regard to the dimensions chiefly operated with being according to the way their twig of personality has been bent in youth or by heredity. Sociologists prefer familiar backgrounds, anthropologists strange, remote, exotic, or ancient ones. Anthropologists tend to be original romantics—even if often disciplined ones—with an esthetic-sensory ingredient prominent; sociologists are intellectually oriented and theoretical formulations come more readily to them. They are at home in the contemporary and content with it, whereas many anthropologists, especially when archaeologists and ethnolinguists are counted in, are stirred by curiosity about the past. All these polarities seem to rest more on temperament than on principle. But they lead to preoccupation with different kinds of materials requiring each its own techniques and usually furthering separate types of problems.

There is, however, one area in which sociological theory and anthropological theory do look in opposite directions. This is the area of social structures and action. This the anthropologist construes as outrightly a part of cultural structure and cultural behavior. In other words, he sees human societal phenomena as simply one segment of culture, entirely coördinate with the subsistence, technological, aesthetic, and religious segments of culture. Such an attitude is pragmatically justified: anthropologists have been successfully dealing with social organization and activity in just this way for a century. On the contrary, nearly all sociologists accord a definite primacy to social aspects within the sociocultural field. The nonsocietal parts of culture—like technology and religion—are seen by them as a sort of extension of the societal, as somehow flowing from it. This view also works pragmatically. To be sure, the particular forms of, say, religions can hardly be derived or historically explained from particular societal forms. But then, sociologists do not ordinarily so derive them, or concern themselves with the form and content of particular religions, but limit themselves to the societal relations and functions of religion. And they have at least this to justify their primacy of valuation: in evolution, societies arise far earlier than man. On the other hand, culture is made possible by peculiar superadded faculties, and these contribute more richly to full human realization than do the strictly societal impulses and endowments which men so largely share with many subhuman species.

X

As for economics and politics, which with sociology constitute the main mass of the core of social science, they are cultural in that they deal each with a segment of culture. They are also societal or social in that they are *de facto* concerned largely with interpersonal relations and behavior within the frame of their particular cultural segment. Most significantly, however, economics and politics seem to be applied or practical sciences. Or it might be fairer to say that they currently pass as having utility, and deal with aspects of life which are inescapable and therefore of practical import. Economics is older than either sociology or anthropology, or for that matter than autonomous psychology. Politics or government is not; but then the older economics was political economy.

It is quite evident that economics did not grow as a direct offshoot of natural science, either organic or inorganic. It grew in essential independence of them, as both its original and its present content indicate. Nor, though younger than the humanities, is economics an offshoot from these: it contains nothing of them nor has it ever claimed to be a humanity. It obviously sprang—and as an unusually autonomous approach—from something in the nature of its age and its area—the age and area of the incipient industrial revolution. There just had come to be more economic behavior there and then, and of greater variety, strength, and influence, than before; and the science of economics developed as its intellectual reflection. It described and analyzed the many new and important facts of economic behavior in northwestern Europe around the turn of the eighteenth century. This pragmatic origin accounts for the separateness, the almost isolationism, of the science. Economic theory really circumscribes its field in such a way as to insulate it: it does not bring economics into wider relation with the remainder of science.

Pointing in the same direction are the early quantification and use of statistics in economics. This seems not to have been in imitation of physics as a model, as it was so largely when psychology and sociology began to quantify. It seems due to the fact that wealth is itself conspicuously quantitative, that money is a natural quantitative index, and that bookkeeping, taxes, tariffs, and population are inevitable materials for census and statistical treatment to a far greater degree than almost all other human behavioral activities.

Economics is therefore only to a slight and indirect extent a branching out of the current of total science—as by contrast sociology at least wanted to believe itself to be. Economics stood solidly on its own sturdy feet from the beginning; and it remains conspicuously uninfluenced by concepts of general science, such as physiological reactions, evolution, genetics, culture, the unconscious.

The so-called political science of government was constituted much later than economics, its national organization in America being formed only around the turn of the last century, synchronously with those of sociology and anthropology. Political science grew out of modern and contemporary history, and the dividing line between them has never become sharp, transitions of personnel still occurring. There is also little material, specific and particular to political study, and little quantification. Documents still prevail as in history.

XI

When it comes to what are known as humanistic studies, it is clear that they control large areas of our knowledge of man with a singular intensity and devotion; yet they jealously resist incorporation into total science. Their faces are turned against integration with biology or even with any body of knowledge that recognizes a biological fundament. Overwhelmingly, they continue to reject measurement. Where the social sciences have often shown insecurity by hastily grasping at measurement and experiment and trying to follow physics as a model, the humanities have tended to act as if physics did not exist—nor for that matter the earth and life sciences. They have accumulated great masses of concrete, highly individualized, and accurate knowledge about human beings and their behavior, especially about men of the past; but they have remained chary of generalization and averse to larger systematized theory either of their own or that derived from natural science. Humanists have been censured for backwardness in learning the coöperative, mass-production methods of modern laboratory science, but unfairly so: at their best they are not technicians who can be turned out by specification of measure, but master craftsmen respecting their own integrity. And, broadly speaking, they have never forced false unions or merely verbal junctions.

Nevertheless, it is plain that such a large part of the area of knowledge of man as the humanities control cannot be permanently reserved as outside natural science. Man *is* in nature even if he does also have a history. The totality of natural science eventuates variegatedly according to both subject matter and method of approach. The humanists are right that every genuine approach is legitimate, and must be developed by those who adhere to it, rather than by any predetermined uniform plan. Also, their disdain of premature theorizing is to be commended. Yet there can be no permanent exclusion of any field of knowledge from generalizing interpretation, especially from interpretations linked to other interpretations.

It seems exceedingly doubtful that the majority of humanists still believe in spirit or spirituality except as a metaphor, or that they hold to the existence of the human soul alongside the natural world but unaffected by it. Nevertheless, they act, on the whole, as if they clung to such belief—or at least to old rights of exclusiveness established when the belief prevailed. Nor can the absolute norms for which they still sometimes make claims be sacredly preserved from analysis and comparative weighting—though it is, of course, everyone's privilege to adhere to and practice any norm he wishes. But science which is natural science can recognize no limits except where phenomena end.

This was not always true. Even in the realm of the physical, it is only a few centuries ago that science in Europe stood under the censorship of theology; and after that day had passed, there was still a period when habits or taste kept the entrance to certain areas of personality, of values, of ethics locked against science. And perhaps science itself felt too unsure, or too preoccupied with fields more peacefully productive, and so did not press too seriously for entry. Yet that time being over, the humanities must obviously abandon their remnants of chauvinism, isolationism, and normation, and recognize the freedom of movement and residence of all citizens of knowledge.

In return, humanists will be welcome in the camp of natural science. After all, they value clarity and precision and have a genuine respect for fact. And the historical approach which humanists so largely employ is finding increasing use and understanding in the natural sciences, so that humanists will not seem there like men marked apart by strange apparel and manners.

Of all the humanities at present, linguistics is perhaps the nearest in method and attitude to a natural science. If scientists claimed annexation of this field as theirs, linguists would soon feel at home. The nature of language is such that it is unusually well set apart within human behavior, and its forms are more regular and significant than its content or meaning. Linguists, therefore, have the sense of patterning well developed, and are skillful in it in ways and degrees analogous to those of biologists and chemists.

They are familiar with historical, with analytical, and with comparative approaches. They have recently purified their method of operating with pattern by excluding from consideration everything nonformal, even the psychological and cultural elements that obviously are present in linguistic phenomena. The findings are little else than a series of models. This phase of linguistic development has probably more or less reached its climax and will be succeeded by one of broadening of base; but it has carried linguistics to a high degree of refinement which will earn the respect of physicists when they learn to understand the operations in the linguistic field, as well as perhaps serving as a model for other humanistic branches in a foreseeable rapprochement.

I have faith that the meeting and gradual federative union of natural science and humanities will begin to occur soon, smoothly and more fruitfully than is generally assumed.

XII

I have said little about integration. It is a much abused word in science. It has acquired fetishistic value, and is often vainly claimed or hollowly forced. To recognize integration where it is really present is one of the fundamental aims of knowledge; but to recognize the areas in which it has not been found, or is perhaps nonexistent, is an equal responsibility. Monism may have justification; but again it has been held to in satisfaction of an emotional yearning, of an infantile craving for simplicity, while reality remains complex and plural. A pantheistic belief that world, god, and soul are one is a good basis for a religion; but as a premise it would soon choke specific curiosity and science to death.

I hold it as a virtue of my own profession of anthropology that it possesses strong integrative drives; for instance, the need to see cultures as wholes as well as analytically, and beyond that at least to adumbrate an understanding of human culture as an historic totality. These are large tasks, we are a small group, and it behooves us not to be arrogant, but to seek and stimulate allies who, if they are like-minded, can accomplish far more than we could unaided.

At the same time culture is a distinctive and unique aspect of man whose distinctiveness must be fully recognized if it is to be fully understood. Culture rests on society, on the individual personality and species, on a long and continuing history of life; and for full apprehension it will ultimately have to be brought into full relation with all these. There is no reason why this integration should not be envisaged and begun now, provided the further prosecution of inquiry into culture as such is not thereby suspended or abrogated, but is indeed developed. For analysis is as important as synthesis, and distinction of the particular and unique is as important as its integration. Synthesis is the larger achievement and a wished-for goal; but it is analysis that not only makes genuine synthesis possible but also renders it meaningful.

9. What Ethnography Is

By usage rather than definition, ethnography deals with the cultures of the nonliterate peoples.

The time is past when peoples and races could be confounded in a scholarly context. Race is a biological concept, people a social concept. Occasionally a race and a people coincide; sometimes they overlap; always they are distinct aspects of human populations.

In a strictly social sense, peoples are the units into which the population of an area is grouped—its bands, tribes, nations, or stocks. These may or may not have native names; their cohesiveness may be weak and transient or strong and enduring; but always there is a degree of cohesiveness—of in-group recognition—by definition. The determination and classification of the sociopolitical groups of an area are necessary for identification of whose history and qualities it is that are being studied ethnographically. In themselves, however, such identifications have a relatively narrow and special factual interest: they lend themselves readily to speculations as to "origin" (which usually is undiscoverable with certainty) and on connections, but hardly to broader conceptual formulations. Keane, Radcliffe-Brown, and some others have tried to make historical ethnology consist wholly of such searches or speculations as to tribal or national

---

Reprinted by permission from *Ethnographic Interpretations 1-6*, University of California Publications in American Archaeology and Ethnology, Vol. 47, No. 2 (1957), 191-204.

identities. This is a gratuitous view and a depreciatory one. It leaves culture out, in order to reserve it to the seekers of laws of social structure.

The culture of a population or society is evidently a matter of greater import, a larger and more significant thing, than the origin and migrations of the population, its alternating coalescence and redivision into tribes, nations, or other groups.

The culture is the distinctive ways of behaving of a group and its distinctive products—its customs, beliefs, ideals, and achievements. Its culture is what a society can leave behind it after the society is dissolved away or absorbed. It is what the society contributes to the history of the world. Essentially, or most significantly, ethnography is concerned with cultures, even if mainly they be those of a lower order.

In principle, the cultures of the world, past and present, form an interconnected continuum, and it is somewhat arbitrary to dichotomize this continuum on the one specific issue of whether particular cultures do or do not have writing, and to call them civilized or uncivilized accordingly. However, our minds are so constituted that they like such big, sweeping bisections; and while it is of course ordinarily less sound, because less in accord with the usage of natural science, to base classification on one characteristic than on many, it must yet be admitted that if we do limit ourselves to one criterion, it is hard to see which distinction within human culture would be more significant than that of literacy.

At any rate, it is with writing that history can begin to be recorded, and some degree of the practice of historical recording does usually soon follow. History, as actually practiced, can be defined—not too amissly—as that branch of learning which deals with written documents about those actions of men which are also social events or result in general conditions.

Ethnography, on the other hand, does not find its documents; it makes them, by direct experience of living or by interview, question, and record. It aims to grasp and portray sociocultural conditions: merely summarized at first, and often moralized, as by Tacitus and Herodotus; but, with luck, proceeding in some degree to treat of recent individuals also. It can occasionally deal with persons who lived as far back as Napoleon is from us, but probably never as remote as Luther, because without documents history rapidly dissolves into culturally patterned fictive creations. We call these creations legends and myths, and they have ethnographic and almost always some literary value, but their historical validity diminishes with each generation at an exponential rate.

The result is that ethnography primarily portrays conditions of a moment, or culture seen synchronically, as a people's culture is organized into more or less coherent patterns. The staticness of such a view is transcended in two ways: microscopically and telescopically.

The microscopic approach adds "depth" to the basic culture patterns, embroidering or enriching them through interest in persons and their motivations, and in pertinent individual events. This predilection also enables short-term changes of culture to be observed and partly analyzed in terms of individual influences. With individuals and motivations deliberately included, a color of personality psychology is imparted to the results; which, however, most psychologists regard as at most a marginal tincturing by their subject. The observing of individually motivated actions also allows of a causal or dynamic interpretation being given to the flow of culture. Such a dynamic presentation can be called "historical" because it records change as well as pattern. It is, however, a very brief-term history that is obtained in this way, because of the fallaciousness of interpersonal memory unsupported by written records. Nor may such a one-generation-long "history" be taken as typical and repetitive, because while basic human nature is undoubtedly repetitive, the very change observed results in altered culture patterns, in which the repeating human nature must operate differently; not to mention broad superpersonal influences—environmental, populational, contact with cultures of different antecedents—which may never be permanently disregarded. Every historian knows intuitively that no one generation or segment of history can ever be accepted as being exactly repeated elsewhere, or even of having its particular combination of activating processes repeated.

Instead of refocusing from the culture of a society to the persons involved in it, the telescopic approach gathers in other cultures and compares them with one another as cultures, with emphasis both on exact feature of pattern ("typology") and on occurrence in geography ("distribution"). In this way a degree of long-range historical reconstruction can be effected for specific items of culture. However, features of culture are potentially so independent of one another—paper manufacture is transmitted by China to Europe, but type printing is not—that these special histories of fragments of culture add up very slowly and imperfectly to generalized histories of whole cultures. It is true that typology and distribution will yield probable classifications of cultures which carry considerable historical implications. But historians are wary of or discontent with mere implications, and scholars intent on demonstration of causal mechanisms are impatient of classification.

It has become clear that in this matter of a reconstruction of the larger and long-range movements or developments in global human culture, the ethnographer or ethnologist needs the help of the archaeologist. The ultimate purposes of the two are the same: to discover the history or evolution of culture; but their instruments and methods are quite different. The archaeologist also operates with typologies and distribution, but he adds a third procedural mechanism not open to the ethnologist, to whom it is an end but cannot be a means: namely chronology, or distribution in time. Relative distribution in time is what the archaeologist can hope to discover by his own archaeological techniques; but these results are then often potentially convertible into absolute

WHAT ETHNOGRAPHY IS

time, either by cross-secting with inscriptions or the datings of history, or by calling in the aid of techniques from the underlying botanical, geological, chemical, or nuclear physical sciences, such as coördinated counts of tree rings, varves, chlorine, or carbon-14 residues.

The archaeologist's data consist of preserved objects, especially cultural products, plus information on their position, topologically and geographically. Both these sets of data are objective, and if sufficiently numerous and precise they are incontrovertible. They also contain subjectively apprehensible information, for instance on style qualities and style changes. And they allow of inferences on the conversion of space relations into time relations of relative sequence. Archaeology accordingly is by nature strong where ethnology is weakest—in the objectivity of its data and in direct historicity—although it is restricted to securing immediate data on only part of any total culture. The two approaches supplement each other so gratifyingly because they approach a common purpose with quite distinct methods.

What the ethnographer is alone in doing within the "social sciences," and almost alone in anthropology as the word is used in English, is two things. He tends to envisage his problems or objectives holistically; and he prefers to acquire his data by holistic contact, person to person, face to face, by word of mouth plus his own observation. This last is not ordinarily true in history, study of government, economics, or sociology, where already compiled documents, censuses, codes, trade reports, and such are the usual primary sources of information. Sociology alone supplements these in considerable degree with the questionnaire, a document elicited in individual manifold, but extracted with minimum or no direct personal contact, and necessarily subtending a rather narrow angle.

As we have already said, the ethnographer makes his documents as he works. He knows their occasion and context, he can more or less judge their bias, he can extend or reduce the scope of his inquiry, he can return with fresh insight to recommence it.

In entering upon an uninvestigated people or topic, he is literally enjoying satisfactions of discovery and charting new terrains of knowledge—activities at least akin to creativity. Even where he has had predecessors, there usually remain new extensions and supplements to be made. The choices whether to turn here or there, where to extend and where to intensify understanding, are manifold, are exhilarating like all discovery, and call for alert mobility and generalized resourcefulness rather than steady, orderly progression, though considerable overarching patience is also a desideratum. If inquiries are pursued with tact to avoid engendering needless fears or hostility, they can go on almost endlessly. Novel situations are always turning up, and there are ever further informants to be tapped who are specialists in some domain of their culture, or who can ably express their world view.

Just as there are no natural stopping places, once one has embarked on uncovering an unknown language, until its limits are reached, so with a culture. The freedom of the person-to-person approach somehow leaves the investigator always aware of the larger whole in which the items he has so far acquired are imbedded. And while he senses that he may never attain complete control of the totality, its relevance is constantly obtruded. Thus the method of acquiring information, and the tendency to deal with cultural wholes, go hand in hand.

In recent decades there has been an inclination to shift ethnographic studies from Tikopians, Hopi, Nuer, and other nonliterates and primitives to linguistically or geographically defined communities within literate civilizations. It is evident that this is a transfer of method: the inquiry remains face-to-face and is applied to a totality, but the totality is a sociocultural unit or subunit.

As to the advantage or disadvantage of the transfer to new material, the shift has in its favor that it extends the ethnographic method to fields where it may perhaps always remain subsidiary to dealing with documents already extant, but to which it might certainly make new contributions, whether these be only supplementary or ultimately become primary also. Biologists take for granted that primitive as well as advanced forms, and advanced as well as primitive, must be considered in their endeavors to understand life, even though many techniques and particular problems may differ in the two domains. It would be equally unfortunate to admit only objective documentation as serving understanding of advanced societies and cultures and only subjective observation and recollection for the nonliterates.

Yet it is plain that face-to-face community studies alone will never suffice for an understanding of a culture as large as that of China, of a nation like the French, or even of a smaller one like the Danes. A thousand towns, communes, or parishes known in this way would not add up to knowledge of France or Denmark. Though they might present precious concrete detail and illuminate numerous humble aspects of life remaining subliminal in the documentary records, they would reflect most incompletely, if at all, the larger heightened elements, the most pervasive and general aspects, of the total culture—its national power, leadership, guidance, genius, resource, and achievement.

To this may be added that not only these greater things but the whole of a society and culture are founded in and produced so largely by its past, that an adequate understanding of its present necessarily involves knowledge of its past. To this past, ethnographic primary investigation, being essentially synchronic in its approach, can attain only indirectly and very imperfectly.

There would be something insensate in the notion that any number of "community studies" made by ethnographic field methods could add up to more significant knowledge of France or Denmark—or the United States—than is already available from the social scientists, officials, intelligentsia, and general citizenry of these countries. I do not believe that any of the social anthropologists or sociologists now making such studies delude themselves with the belief that their studies, even in the aggregate, will bring about a revolution of man's understanding of his larger social selves.

Why then the drive to conduct such studies, if at best they only supplement or illustrate larger generalizations obtained in other ways, by adding intimate, close-up, and detailed pictures, of tiny samples of greater fabrics, which it is hoped they may illustrate typically and concretely?

As a matter of fact, to date many more such studies, and allied acculturation studies, have originated in dissertations for the doctorate than have been produced by the scholars who direct and accept such dissertations. The studies can usually be made with little travel and little cost, in one's own country and often in a community that one knows or has lived in. They can ordinarily be conducted in English or among some ethnic minority which one can reach with a language like Spanish, or through American-born Orientals. If the group is an immigrant one, it is not necessary to know the culture of Sweden or Portugal or Greece, but only as much as the immigrants themselves can impart about their former home customs and values—because the subject of a study is not an alteration of the culture of Sweden, but how a group of Swedish peasants, or Greek sponge-fishermen, have adapted to American life. The latter is already familiar; and of what was Swedish or Greek only so much is relevant as the elders in the Greek community recall by way of contrast or have preserved. The requisite equipment of knowledge or method on the part of the investigator is really quite modest. A certain amount of new information is readily acquired, and has the merit of being relatively novel to most readers and of being given a degree of coherence through the fact that it depicts the way of life of a group selected for retaining a measure of coherence. The investment and risks of time and knowledge are really small, but the returns—apart from a probable professional degree—are important to the student in that he enters his profession with a record of "field work done," of having used the face-to-face method of inquiry on a group. Students are quite correct in appreciating the value of having had this experience: it is the crucial hallmark of the anthropological investigator.

It is rarely that community studies get above the descriptive level—a fact which to be sure they share with ethnographic studies of primitives. There is, however, one difference.

An ethnographic description of a primitive people may be performed out of intrinsic interest or a sort of infatuation. Yet it is also a brick that gets built—by others if not by the author—into a structure, namely, the record and understanding of all human culture through time and area, which makes it potentially more than just another tribal ethnography. This is an objective which I want to say more about later; but it is at any rate an end that aims to take us out of ourselves, our day, and our own puddle. In the community study the main result recorded is mostly how others become more like ourselves; which seems an ethnocentrically tinged interest for an anthropologist. There may be compensating motivations and values which I am not the one to discover. If so, I hope some proponent will become eloquent about them.

Acculturation studies in particular, at any rate as they are conducted in America, seem particularly monotonous and depressing, equally so whether the acculturees are ethnic minority immigrants or ethnic remnant aborigines. These unfortunates always emerge from the process as bottom-level members of our own society and culture. Perhaps they are lucky at that: most of the immigrants seem to think so, if most of the Indians do not. Yet each study appears to be the repetition of a principle akin to the one that when a bulldozer meets the soil that nature has been depositing for ages, the bulldozer always and promptly wins.

It is often said that the switch of interest away from primitives to minorities and communities in civilization is due to primitives fast losing their primitiveness or dying out, the world over. This diminution is no doubt actual, but it does not seem to be the main reason for the growing neglect of old-fashioned ethnography. It costs no more in time and money to study the native culture of an Indian tribe as it survives in the memory of the older members than to study the acculturation of their children and grandchildren, or the facet of our own civilization exemplified by a neighboring white community or sect. But the native study does require, as a precondition of success, more knowledge of ethnographic background, and more skill in eliciting significant data. Such knowledge and skill are becoming rarer among our anthropological students. And why should they trouble to acquire them when they receive the same professional certification and recognition for more commonplace knowledge and thinking? Ethnographic descriptions can also be very dull reading even for an anthropologist, if he does not know enough to fit them into an intellectual structure.

This attitude in turn is strengthened by the increasing acceptance of anthropology as a regular member of the social sciences instead of remaining a hard-to-place oddity or an assemblage of somewhat queer specialties. By and large, social scientists and their public have assumed that their studies were useful because they were practical, that they made for the more efficient conduct of public and private affairs. Often they have even intimated that if this were not so, sensible people would not waste effort on social studies. But this was not in the least true of ethnological anthropology in its beginnings, which were a combination of naturalistic and humanistic impulses. However crude its efforts may sometimes have seemed to naturalists and perverted to humanists, those efforts were obviously actuated by intellectual curiosity, by a wish to expand the horizons of understanding, not by any seeking for immediate utilities. With such beginnings, the acceptance and swamping of ethnology and the rest of cultural anthropology by social science aims and attitudes could only result in a dilution, in a lowering of sights from former targets.

From its inception the Social Science Research Council has excluded from its grants support for studies in ethnography, in archaeology, in languages and linguistics, as it has essentially excluded ancient history, non-Occidental civilizations (until the rise of "areal programs"), the development and theory of arts and literatures. Most of these fields have received some encouragement, though out of much more slender resources, from the council of learned societies devoted to the humanities; but ethnography has been omitted by both; and except transiently, by the council for natural sciences. There has been support for ethnography from universities, museums, and special research foundations; and it may perhaps be properly maintained that no vital branch of learning should be too much dependent upon donations. I make no complaints: ethnography survives; I believe it will come into its own in time. But I also believe the Councils must accept partial responsibility for largely overlaying it, during the past three decades, with forms of allied research activity whose targets were more immediate and intellectually humbler.

Some special relations of ethnography to fields of study wholly or partly outside the social sciences deserve consideration.

Psychology has always been considered wholly nonhistorical in its aims and methods, which are avowedly concerned with process.

Social psychology seems to have grown partly out of an interest in suggestion and suggestibility, imitation and mob influence. It was developed in France by jurists like Tarde and LeBon, in America about equally by sociologists and psychologists, and is still shared here between the two disciplines. It seems characteristic of social psychology that the societies it ordinarily deals with are not units occurring in nature or history, or determinate by definition, but *ad hoc* units, varying with the situation. This would mean that the real topic considered is interpersonal influences, multiple or singular, rather than the relation of the individual to the social unit as a natural or historic phenomenon.

The largest unit which straight psychology treats holistically is the organic individual. Even this unit is usually dealt with only in clinical or psychiatric or personality psychology, which differs from all the rest of psychology in being nonexperimental and nonquantitative. It is essentially this personality psychology that has been injected into the study of culture in recent years.

If this is the essential situation, then psychology, after detaching itself from philosophy and setting out to be an experimental and quantitative natural science dealing with precisely defined and narrow fields, strictly controllable, has now let itself be led to a considerable extent into the realm of social science, whereas the largest unit with which it, *qua* psychology, actually operates, still is the individual person.

I do not understand this contradiction, except that the given material of psychology evidently is unusually recalcitrant to fertile natural science treatment. The yield of ore seems to run low per ton of effort. The results do not appear to add up to much wide significance—in situations selected for their testability; especially not accumulatively. On the contrary the one method of psychological thought that has proved originative and fruitful, the Freudian, is untestable scientifically, the line of division in it, between what is probable and instrumentally useful or merely speculatively possible, having to be made by common-sense human experience.

Incidentally, Freud's and his successors' ventures into the causality of culture are now generally accepted as in the second category. On the other hand, his generally accepted insights do bear at least on the life history of the individual. It may be argued that so repetitive and minimal a "history" as this, is not really history at all, in the sense that we can speak of the history of a species, or of life on our earth, or the history of the earth's crust, or of the solar system. There is certainly a difference here. And if my doubts are accepted and sustained—that a life history is not significant history but is exemplary definition of recurrent types —like cells or crystals or pebbles—then the reason for psychology remaining wholly nonhistorical is the sound one that the historical potentialities of psychological phenomena already find expression in documentary history, ethnography, archaeology, and the social sciences generally so far as these do not aim at being "nomothetic."

Only, in that event, the formulation of the relation of psychology to natural and to social science is in current need of revised definition.

Linguistics is almost always reckoned a humanity, although in precision and rigor of techniques and breadth of fundamental method it probably transcends all other humanistic and social studies. At that it is only now manifesting the first impulses toward quantitative analysis; it has mainly operated with qualitative precision of definition of pattern, sharpened in recent decades by successful use of the principle of contrast. I accept Hockett's definition of linguistics as a natural history of languages. It uncovers patterns that exist in speech, although for the most part covertly and unconsciously, and that allow considerable degree of predictability as to elements present but not yet discovered.

Philological linguistics is distinguished from general linguistics by restriction to concern with written languages and by association with literary problems; also, in the past, often by normative interests. It also began, nearly two centuries ago, to work out the comparative history of the Indo-European languages, and later of other ethnic groups having each a common speech origin.

General linguistics is interested in the pervading principles to be found—with enormous variation in detail—in all the languages of mankind. Every language is therefore an exemplification, to greater or less degree, of particular or novel patterns of structure, quite independent of the number of its speakers, their importance in history, their literary or other cultural achievements. On examination a language may prove to be as distinctive from everything previously described as a kiwi or platypus, or as unexpectedly out of place as a marsupial opossum in America. This comparison may validate the appellation of linguistics as a "natural history."

The recording and description of never-before-written languages had of course to be devised gradually, much as were ethnographic approaches and renderings. It pays to remember, however, that the beginning had to be made by starting with the scripts and grammatical concepts of the "high" languages of philology, and that analytical originality of an elevated order was involved in the first grammars extricated, those of Sanskrit and then of Greek. All subsequent language descriptions were patterned on these—if soundly done, with reformulation of pattern instead of its mere repetitive application.

The description of previously undescribed languages carried the process a step farther, especially when all the speakers were illiterate; and the outcome has been a reconceptualization of the range of elements and forms of language, which has allowed philologists to distinguish better between what is intrinsic form and what the caked scum of idiosyncratic history, in the presentation of the languages of high civilization. Thus general linguists and philologists are less far apart than sometimes still seems to them.

In the gathering of data on newly discovered languages, ethnologists took part with ardor from the first. From the time anthropology was first conceived as a unified field of inquiry by Tylor and then by the organizing founders like Powell and Brinton in America, language has always been recognized as an integral part of this field, specially associated with ethnography; and cultural anthropologists like Boas and Sapir have been influential in pure linguistics, and their students after them. Linguists on their side can fairly be said to recognize language as within culture, though as constituting a domain which can be autonomously treated.

Reconstruction of an earlier or "original" form of several languages now diverse but still related has long been practiced on Indo-European, then on other families of Old World languages of which at least some had been written. Such reconstruction is now in full swing for a number of aboriginal families in America, all of them unwritten by their own speakers. Thirty years ago I called attention to the fact that by contrast, reconstruction of former cultures was often being frowned upon in ethnography. The reason for the difference is more easily seen now: the patterns of language are sharper and can be defined with less residue, perhaps because they come more interwoven in a semiautonomous nexus. Geographic and social environment impinges more heavily on culture, and this therefore normally contains more nonconformable components.

Linguists are also more rigorous in not commingling synchronic and diachronic treatments. Both treatments are legitimate to them; but the problems are different—statically descriptive as against comparative or dynamically historical—and therefore best kept separate. Ethnographers would do well to observe the same distinction throughout—we do in some measure. It is enough to recall for instance how infantile the attempts of Cushing seem today who thought he could explain the causal origin of almost any interesting phenomenon he encountered.

Bloomfield is still being followed by nearly all linguists, at least in America, in "casting out mentalism." Not that anyone claims that there is no psychology involved in language, but that the business of the linguist is the discernment and interrelating of the forms of languages, and that the causal explanation of these in psychological terms is the business of psychologists and is best left to them. This principle has been much less straightly announced and followed by ethnographers for culture, but tacitly it is being observed considerably. Few ethnologists today would account for cultural forms by unblushing appeal to psychology as Tylor and Frazer did. We might be more likely to bring "human nature" into a situation to suggest where one cultural form finds an inherent limit, or why another conceivable form fails to occur at all.

Psychologists on their part seem quite unable to bring their resources to bear to achieve anything with either linguistic or cultural forms. For instance, a broad and positive result of modern linguistics is that the basic units of speech are the phoneme and the morpheme. The syllable is recognized, but secondarily and incidentally. On the other hand, in the historic devising of phonetic writing and in metrics, two activities which are perhaps essentially cultural though resting directly on language in that they operate with linguistic forms, the syllable is important but the phoneme and morpheme are incidental. These are positive findings from a growing series of historically attested cases, with few or no exceptions. The reasons are not known. Linguists and ethnologists could guess at them but do not. Psychologists might conceivably know or devise an attack on the problem; but they have not done so in my cognizance. In fact, modern psychology seems unable or unwilling to come to grips with any established phenomena in the wider history of mankind. This is of course in line with its genuine antihistoricity, its feeling that to become scientific it must avoid traffic with qualitative forms. It is only within the very last few years that efforts have been made from psychology to approach language, and they are still limited.

Another element that general linguistics is trying to eliminate as far as possible is meaning. It is recognized that this cannot be wholly dispensed with—separate elements that are homonymous would be treated as one, if it were omitted—but meaning is left out where it may be omitted. This is again a sharpening of objective and method. Meaning is not denied of course: it is only treated as intrinsically irrelevant to the working out of relations of linguistic form. This ignoring obviously cannot be continued indefinitely; sooner or later there will have to be reassociation of aspects that occur associated in the phenomenon. But meanwhile their discrimination makes progress possible.

Here again ethnography, though dealing with analogous and related phenomena, lags behind. It is not even clear precisely what the cultural counterpart of linguistic meaning is. It is obviously somewhere in the range of *use, meaning,* and *function* as these were distinguished from one another and from *form* by Linton and then by Homer Barnett. But no student of culture seems as yet to have discovered how to make really operational and constructive use of this fourfold discrimination. At any rate, we do

WHAT ETHNOGRAPHY IS

not know what we would cast out if we wanted to emulate the linguists. My unsure guess is that it would first of all be *function*, which looks suspiciously like a covert or ulterior *purpose;* perhaps cultural *meaning*, also, whose boundary with function runs somewhat fluid.

A last new method of linguistics that as yet has no counterpart in ethnography is glottochronology, or lexicostatistics used as a measure of time lapse. This is still under fire from most general linguists; but they are slowly giving ground, and in a limited way some of them are beginning to use the method. The procedure rests on the assumption that the rate of linguistic change is constant, or perhaps that among the factors which produce linguistic changes there is one factor that is a constant. This working hypothesis has not been proved, but the assumption has the merit of arousing interest, so that in five or ten years it may be proved or disproved, or we shall know better how far it is true. There may be too many conjoined variables to allow the absolute age of separateness of languages to be reliably computed, as has been hoped by some. But it seems already reasonably sure that the method will yield at least a relative time classification or phylogeny within groups of languages visibly akin as members of a family.

The analogous assumption might profitably be made for culture, if anyone could devise a technique. The devising would obviously be more difficult. Language is a smaller part of "total culture," more narrow in the range of its phenomena, and more autonomous than the remainder; its forms, as already said, are sharper in definition; and certain operations are therefore more easily carried out on linguistic phenomena. The more reason why students of culture should watch its developments and successes.

So much for linguistics; except for one general remark. It is clear that it began its separation from philology by making discriminations of subject and method and adhering to them, and that it has continued to find and observe new distinctions as it progressed. If such is a road of scientific development, it carries a suggestion for ethnography and all other studies concerned with culture: to distinguish conceptually with clarity the social aspects from the cultural within the sociocultural range, and to be ready, whenever the phenomena or the situation allow, to deal separately with them for greater intellectual advance. Resynthesis can come later, and will come if it is feasible; but there can be no resynthesis made of elements or qualities imperfectly discriminated.

I have said that I consider ethnography a natural science dealing for the most part with phenomena usually assigned to the humanities. More exactly it would be a form of natural history, or scientific description, narration, and classification. In precision, too, as long as ethnography is restricted to phenomena from nonliterary cultures, it cannot be said to deal with wholly humanistic materials—only with data which, if they had emanated instead from literate cultures, especially certain ethnocentrically approved ones, would then be construed as humanistic.

Considering myself half humanist in spiritual ancestry and proclivities, I proceed to try to define the relations that exist and should exist between cultural anthropology, of which ethnography is probably the core, and the humanities. In principle I see no difference: We are all concerned with the products of human culture, big or little, developed or rudimentary; with special emphasis on creative products. As part of this concern we deal with the discernment, discrimination, formulation, comparison, and history of values. I hold that such concern with values is potentially a natural history of values, and actually becomes such as soon as the base of consideration is broad enough to include *all* values as phenomena, subject as are other phenomena of culture, to analysis and comparison without normative coloration or reservation. What that attitude however does exclude is normative activities which aim to withdraw certain phenomena from analysis and comparison. I suspect that more humanists than is ordinarily thought would subscribe to some such creed as this. In any event, we are not far apart.

The natural history to which I see ethnographic activity related is theoretically that of the human animal. But this being imperfect, fragmentary, and disturbed, and human history substituting for it inadequately by limiting itself, to date, unduly to the documentary, the natural history of the animal kingdom must partly take its place. Considerable as is the distance between a single species with speech and culture and all other animal species without, the real rapport of ethnography seems to me for the present to lie with animal structure and behavior rather than with human psychology in its momentary disappointingly limited phase.

The difference in this respect between zoölogical science and psychology appears to be one of degree of orderly development and organization. Zoölogy began with description and went on to classification on a broad base: configurative, anatomical, and behavioral description and classification of the entire kingdom so far as known. Knowledge of physiological processes, which are largely internal, followed later, and reached full development with laboratory experiment and linkage with chemistry. Then came the revolutionizing idea that the whole array of life did not have to be viewed only statically, but could and must be seen dynamically, diachronically, also; what had been mere classification therewith became an evolution as well. But without the classification having been worked out before—and as a "natural" classification, that is, one derived from and conforming to the totality of the phenomena instead of from ideas derived independently of the phenomena—without this previous taxonomy, Darwin would have been unable to substantiate the origin of species as effectually as he did, nor in fact could he have thought about it fruitfully. But with a vast and ordered array of information at hand when the nineteenth century finally got ready to venture on a diachronic view, the issue was swiftly decided once it was seen that the old static classification was not destroyed but was largely comfortable to the new dynamic point of view. It was like a nation's marshaled army going over to a revolutionary cause.

Then, when a generation later the idea of genetics and the first evidence for it were rediscovered, there was the same body of ordered biological knowledge—considerably increased, in fact—

available as a foundation and soil for the new science to grow in. Besides its novel point of view, genetics introduced experiment of a new though simple type; yet all its successful proliferation rested upon the previous, ordered body of knowledge of biological forms.

Even the Darwinian revolution could not have happened in classical times, in spite of Aristotle and Lucretius having entertained the germinal idea, because the relevant knowledge was too meager and miscellaneous, so that the seed was unable to sprout even in its authors' minds.

Possession of an organized corpus of knowledge of phenomena is the precondition of any soundly growing science. The first step after the acquisition of new knowledge is its ordering or classification. In fact the very ordering will induce further acquisitions, by revealing what seem to be gaps or, on the other hand, growing points. We need not worry too much about interpretation: it will always be attempted. Much of the first interpretations will be imperfect; but they will grow cumulatively in soundness and insight with the body of information.

The distinction is false, both in natural science and in humanistics, between a higher theoretical understanding and a lower order of merely informational knowledge. The one does not grow without the other. True, new ideas are rarer than new facts, and harder to develop or acquire; but there are more facts, and more are needed. To originate a new idea, to observe a novel distinction, is no doubt a more creative act of intellection, and one we all would take more pride in having achieved, than to find and report an indefinite number of new phenomenal items. But science is the interaction of the two things and therefore needs both. And I am of course speaking only of natural science, not of poetry, philosophy, or even mathematics.

How about the corpus of knowledge assembled by ethnography?

It is obviously smaller than that of zoölogical science. But there have been fewer workers, and some of those more given to ideological distraction than is wont in zoölogy. But it is a growing body of information, and increasingly coherent. We cannot be too boastful about it but need not be apologetic. When I recall the knowledge available in my own field of North American ethnography as I entered it around the turn of the century, there were far more gaps than content. Our total positive knowledge now is several times as great, and the areas of total absence of exact information are much shrunken. Continuity of knowledge is much more adequate. Ordering and understanding have kept pace, whether in terms of segments of culture, of spatial distribution, or of historic developments and successions. In this last domain, once American archaeology found itself and faced the time factor, some thirty years ago, progress has been phenomenal.

In one respect we lag behind the biologists owing to a difference in our subject matter. The history of life is like an ever-branching tree. Once life forms have differentiated beyond a certain narrow limit, they cannot reunite. The direction of their evolution may alter, but its continuity is irreversible. A form may die out, or persist, or branch into several, but it does not merge. There are millions of lines of descent in the history of life, but each has been neat and distinct, if we can only recover the facts about it. But in culture we get constant fusing as well as separation. Lines split, but also merge, and the actual course of events is therefore far more intricate, its conceptual representation more complex.

On the other hand, biologists are thrown on their own resources for exact data, but ethnographers and cultural anthropologists can draw help and sustenance from almost all segments of the humanities. Wherever humanistic knowledge and understanding are being acquired, we can enormously profit by their use, whether it be in straight history, art or religious or institutional history, or the history of languages.

10. An Anthropologist Looks at History

THE WRITING of history is perhaps the oldest of scholarly pursuits. Moreover, it has persisted with minimal alteration for more than two thousand years, and across change of language, ever since Herodotus and Thucydides and the even earlier days of the Chinese. History therefore contains much that is art: the narration of significant events in literary prose. This is evident further in the fact that the great historians are also, in the main, great writers. They write the language of total and dignified communication of their day, without technical terms or jargon, less even than philosophers employ. And they operate with a nontechnical psychology, a psychology of generic experience and common understanding. And similarly they operate with an untechnical common man's causality, intelligible on its face; and a similar common morality. Basically, this still holds true as it did two or more millennia ago.

Anthropology is not wholly a historical science, but large areas of it are historical in interest and intent. Prehistory is an allied pursuit of knowledge in the classification of disciplines customary in Europe and an outright part of anthropology in American usage. And prehistoric archaeology is of course, in its aim at least, merely history pushed back of writing and documents, whether in Sumeria, Japan, Morocco, South Africa, the Pueblo Indian Southwest, or Peru. Names and identifiable individuals are of necessity missing when the record is of preliterate times; specific events are determinable only now and then; but the residue of possible findings is a sort of condensed social history. We learn of buildings, artifacts, arts, about bones of animals hunted for daily living and of animals reared domesticated. Human bones give us not only some glimpses of the prevalent physique, but methods of burial, and sometimes clear indications of classes and economic differences. If carvings are cultish, they allow of inferences as to religious beliefs and practices; so do temples, shrines, preserved offerings. Excavations and records, made and kept intensively enough, lead to conclusions as to size of community, number of communities in a period, and other demographic information on populations whose ethnic name may be wholly unknown, and whom the prehistorian may have to christen. We know in some cases the approximate proportion of males and females, of aged and adults and children in a population, and we may be able to speculate with some show of evidence how far its particular distribution of age and sex was due to disease, war, malnutrition, or human sacrifice. All this is most eminently social or cultural history, even though of nameless peoples. In fact, if his luck with the spade is good, the archaeologist may come to control fuller data on daily life and custom than annalists conscious chiefly of kings' glories and battles have left to the historiographer as data for some nominally literate period or country.

Archaeological data resolve naturally into narrative. The very first discoveries in an area may be felt merely as new, different, surprising, or otherwise emotionally toned. But as soon as the remains of the past vary within an area, it is evidently probable that they come from different periods, and intellectual curiosity will try to arrange them in their order of age. Stylistic comparisons, or sometimes typological, sooner or later give clues or indications as to sequences. If ornamented pottery was produced, the task is usually made much easier. Clay is a virtually imperishable material, it is likely to be fairly abundant, it is unusually plastic in its manufacture, and thus if it is decorated its style almost never stands still very long. Many a sequence of pottery styles have been worked out with a fair probability of historic authenticity for societies whose absolute dates we know as little as their names or origins.

The final validation of the archaeologist's reconstructions of the past is by the minutely careful excavation of stratified sites—levels of objects of different style superposed in the sequence of time as they were laid down; like the successive cities of Troy, or the levels of Cnossos. This is the clinching proof. There is an element of luck in the finding of such sites. Peoples of later periods often started to build and live and leave refuse at new sites rather than settle where their predecessors had operated; but not always so; and while discovery of the strategic key site may not be immediate, it is usually located within a generation or two of problem-conscious exploration.

Ways have lately been devised of attaching approximate absolute dates to events and periods established by prehistorians as having occurred in a given relative sequence. Thereby such findings are brought strictly into the compass of history. Dendrochronology or tree-ring dating was the first of these technical methods; it is fully successful, so far, only in certain areas of subnormal rainfall and for certain species of trees. It has carried us back, in our Pueblo-Anasazi Southwest, nearly two thousand years. Carbon-14 determinations reach back from ten to perhaps twenty times as far as dendrochronology. They have solved some chronological problems, have complicated others. They have perhaps helped most in the precopper range of time, and in North America they seem to have halved the estimated time elapsed since the end of the last glaciation, thus yielding a closer tie-up of geology with human prehistory.

Original ethnographic inquiries made by the field anthropologist among surviving native peoples are less patently historical in their immediate results, because of the surprisingly brief historic memories of most nonliterate populations. But here, too, systematic comparison sooner or later leads to perspectives of time depth for institutions, arts, rituals, as for ethnic groups themselves. The ethnographic approach is definitely slower than prehistoric excavation in converting its result into chronologically firm culture history; but it gives a fuller and more living picture because less has been lost by the decays of time.

I think that most anthropologists would look on history as being a realm adjoining their own country, speaking a somewhat different dialect, governed by laws similar in intent though often variant in detail, and connected by innumerable ties of activity across their joint frontier.

I see human history or historiography as a specialization within a much broader and more general intellectual activity: namely, that of viewing any and all phenomena in the universe "historically"—in their flow through time. Just as there legitimately exists "social" and "intellectual" and "economic" history alongside "political" history of the peoples who have left us written documents, so there exists a potential history—in fact an existent and progressive history—of the nonliterate human populations whom we know through their settlements, burials, artifacts, and refuse. There is, further, a history of life. This is the story of biological evolution, as it is now known, both in general outline and—in spots, in considerable detail—from the records of fossils, supplemented by comparisons with the array of living forms of animals and plants. The internal structure and physiology of these living forms being known or ascertainable, they help to illuminate dark areas in the inferences from the fossils. Beyond that there is obviously also a history of our planet as a body; a history of the solar system; and a possible history of galaxies and the universe. These remoter histories may be more largely potentially inferable than already ascertained; but we are here considering what can be done rather than what has been done. And at that, the achieved is considerable—enough to show that we are already far beyond mere vague hopes and dreams.

In short, every part and aspect of our universe has a history which is gradually recoverable. Or let us call it "a historical approach" to the phenomena of primitive man, of life, of the earth, of our solar system. The substitute phrase is suggested to guard against anyone's being worried at stretching the term *history* to a meaning beyond that of the conventional historiography of the written-record-leaving portion of humanity.

My point is that all these interests and inquiries, so far as they aim at narratively understanding a class of phenomena in their flow through time, are of one general kind, of which documented historiography is one particular example, though by far the oldest established example. Why historiography originated two millennia or more earlier than a historical approach in other fields of intellectual inquiry seems to be not at all an insoluble problem, but it is definitely more than can be answered here today. Yet that it originated earlier is an unquestionable fact; and the time available to me may suffice to show, not why human historiography was early, but that the development of the historical approach in other fields of knowledge was on the whole surprisingly late; and perhaps why it was so.

A science like astronomy today has a double aspect. It studies with accuracy and precision the processes that are going on in the universe of the heavens; and it reconstructs the events that have happened in the development of the stars. The Babylonians already, and the Greeks not long after, knew the motions of the planets, the recurring motions and aberrations of the moon, the latitudes and approximate size of the earth. The revolutions of the heavenly bodies were recurrent; they were repeated over and over, identically and endlessly; except for this internal motion, the universe seemed static. It did not appear to have had a history. It seems not even to have occurred to the Greeks that the universe might have had a development. Such motions as they determined and measured, in the great machine of the planetary system, impressed them by their regularity: they were fixed notions: they showed how immutable the machine was; and what is immutable has no history.

Such was still the assumption of Copernicus, two thousand years later. It was not till the eighteenth century that La Place—and the philosopher Kant—originated nebular hypotheses as conjectural histories of how our and other solar systems developed. It took a century and a half of improvement of telescopes and chronometers before enough data had been accumulated on the distances and motions of fixed stars for such hypothetical reconstructions of the history of our universe to be felt as needed and to be devised. In the nineteenth century the spectroscope, photography, and astrophysics have piled up further knowledge, and the histories have been remodeled accordingly.

In other words, here is a precision science, astronomy, quantitative from the first, and cumulatively gaining range and accuracy, which began to see sequential and developmental problems in its material and to find historical answers to them only after more than two millennia of activity.

It was as late as the eighteenth century also that the essentially historical science of geology began dimly to glimpse some ends and tatters of events of our planet's history, in the vulcanist versus neptunist controversy. It was only in the nineteenth century that a reasonably complete sequential series of geologic periods could be laid down.

Biology remained in its totality an ahistorical science until 1859. The efforts of Erasmus, Darwin, Lamarck, and other scattered heretics failed to swerve either botany or zoölogy from regarding their phenomena as essentially fixed and changeless—barring the accidents of occasional catastrophic blottings-out. The entire ramified history of life on earth, as it is accepted by biological consensus today, has been less than a century in its working out. Being worked out as a *story*, that is; for the systematic *classification* of life forms that had been made by and since Linnaeus, supplemented by the discoveries of a hitherto dateless palaeontology, proved to be immediately convertible into a history of life on earth as soon as biologists were ready to think in terms of sequences of events as well as relationship of forms.

It appears from these examples that historiography—the telling of human recorded history—is the only history which is genuinely old as an accepted pursuit; and that the historical sciences are definitely newcomers, both as compared with historiography on the one hand and with mathematics, physics, and astronomy on the other.

Historiography has so consistently been nontheoretical, unwilling or unable to abstract process from out of its phenomena on any notable scale, as to cause the widely prevalent view that history as an endeavor and pursuit *must* be something fundamentally distinct from natural science; or that, if in some measure a science, it was a science of an older and simpler order, forever attached to its phenomena instead of advancing from them to systematic generalization, abstraction, and theory.

Such a view receives surface support from the fact that, as regards both methods and devices used and concepts attained, historiography has essentially stood still while mathematics, astronomy, and physics have cumulatively progressed.

However, if the historical approach were in itself of a simpler order or lower potential than that of systematically conceptual science, we should hardly have historical astronomy, historical geology, and historical biology developing only within the last two centuries.

Accordingly, our problem must evidently be approached in some other way.

I would suggest that in subhuman fields of nature it is naturally easy to recognize repetitive regularities; such as the seasons and the heavenly bodies; the exemplars of a species; such as, also, falling bodies, the action of levers which we daily handle, in fact possess in our limbs; or liquids finding their level. These recurrent regularities in themselves point to law; and the sciences first emanating from them are nomothetic. Natural science thus tends to begin with the static or with motion within a static frame. The longer range macrodynamisms that transform a gaseous nebula into stars and planets, that gradually transmute one kind or order of living things into another, do not obtrude in everyday observation. In fact, they cannot be dealt with, other than by mere speculation, until large masses of observations have been accumulated or wholly new methods of observation have been devised. Hence in the natural sciences of subhuman phenomena the historical approach comes late; it is possible only after much development.

But in men's observations of one another, there is little to lead them to concentrate on recurring regularity or to induce notions of fixity or law. Everyone develops, with the very experience of living, his own practical skills of interpreting and dealing with other human beings, as a practical necessity; but if in spite of this psychology remains the least organized and theoretically least productive of the major sciences, this fact suggests strongly that its material is scientifically the most difficult and recalcitrant. Historiography, however, while it constantly employs unorganized, experientially derived psychological judgments—practical judgments—does not really deal directly with "psyches," as psychology does, but with the multiform actions or events due to these psyches or persons. And in concerning itself with them, it tends to avoid the regular and the expectable, or tacitly takes them for granted, and concentrates on the singular and the unusual, on the stirring and dramatic; and, as it attains to more sophistication, on the significant and effective.

Perhaps if we had a theoretical science of psychology as organized, efficient, and productive on its own level, as are physics, chemistry, and biochemistry, it would be followed before long by a historical psychology corresponding to historical astronomy, geology, and biology. What form such a historical psychology would take, I do not pretend to picture. But it would be interesting to know how far such a scientifically historical psychology would turn out to resemble the history of historians or how far it might transcend it as something radically different in attack, manner, and product.

11. History and Anthropology in the Study of Civilizations

Some General Differences of History and Anthropology

Differences in subject.—History deals with events, with emphasis on uniqueness and on change. Events are the actions of human beings, individually, in groups, or in masses. Anthropology deals primarily with culture, with emphasis on the expectable, on its relatively permanent forms. These are two separate, selective focuses, though many data may be shared.

Differences in method.—History is narrative primarily, with optional halts for "topical" description. This is true by common consent definition. Anthropology is perhaps primarily descriptive (ethnology, ethnography) but also narrative if the data allow— often in most prehistory and archaeology.

Differences in sources.—History relies on written documents, ultimately. Anthropology characteristically "makes" its documents, elicits them in face-to-face situations of oral communication with informants; plus of course observation. In archaeology, physical anthropology, observation is primary.

The face-to-face contacts are almost enforced with primitive cultures, and may have contributed to the further preoccupation

---

Read before the Comparative Civilizations Symposium at the Center for Advanced Study in the Behaviorial Sciences, Stanford, California, spring, 1958.

of ethnology with the primitive. At any rate, anthropologists are often considered romantics among men of science.

Note:—Here, and in what follows, the word "Anthropology" is used in its older and original sense of a widely inclusive science, attempting to understand and interrelate all principal aspects of mankind, with central emphasis on man's most distinctive product, namely culture. The other social sciences are concerned with particular aspects of human culture: social, economic, political, personal. Anthropology alone tries to deal with culture as such, both through total descriptions and through conceptualization, "theoretically." Associated with understanding of culture are knowledge of its past (prehistory); of the most autonomous special sector of culture, namely language; and even of the racial physiques and bodies of men that have produced culture (physical anthropology). The two first of these associated studies—archaeology and linguistics—are usually considered humanities, when pursued in isolation; analogously, racial anthropology is obviously also part of biology. No other social science allows its operations to extend so far into frankly humanistic or natural science. This anomaly of anthropology is undoubtedly connected with its other anomalous feature in the social sciences, its holistic instead of segmental interest in culture. Its holism is almost certainly what for several generations kept anthropology from attempting practical applications.

This is the older and most characteristic form of anthropology, which I am comparing with history.

A more special development began as "functionalism" in England about forty years ago and has gradually assumed the name "Social Anthropology." This sometimes shifts the focus from holistic culture to its societal segment (Radcliffe-Brown) or sometimes uses culture as a base or background against which societal structure and dynamics, interpersonal interactions, and modifications of culture resulting from societal and personal situations, are examined (Firth and others). It is evident that social anthropology is much less anomalous as a social science than was the older anthropology; it is no longer culture-centered and it is no longer actively holistic. In fact, in England, social anthropology, prehistory, and physical anthropology are increasingly prosecuted as separate disciplines, as compared with Tylor's days or even Marett's; and linguistics is not pursued at all, except as a tool, or as a wholly independent study. In the United States, there is little tendency toward separatism, and cultural ("ethnological") and social anthropology are practiced side by side, sometimes even without much awareness of difference.

It is clear that the close-range focus of social anthropology does not encompass large changes and that so far as the results are historical they are characteristically short-term. A comparison with historiography would therefore be limited essentially to "contemporary history."

For this reason the comparisons here made with history are of the culture-centered, holistic, and long-range anthropology which first crystallized out as a discipline and has determined its characteristic trend.

Some Generic Similarities of History and Anthropology

1. Histories generally began on a national, perhaps provincial, basis, but early showed some leanings to being international within a period (Polybius) or civilization, or even to covering all known time and area ("world history"). Anthropological inquiry also varies in range from intensive tribal studies to synthetic ethnographies of the world, and to disquisitions on the nature and properties of culture in general. Both disciplines can take on the long-range and wide view, or the close-up and detailed; both may be holistic but are not necessarily so.

There is one area in which they meet: that of comparative culture history. This involves the comparative running down, across nations and civilizations, of some segment of human activity—a religious form, a mechanical invention, a technological art, a game or an etiquette, an iconography, a philosophical idea, or a symbol. These may be shared by great civilizations with lowly tribal cultures; and the historian of science or art, the Sinologist, classicist, or mediaevalist, share in the search with ethnologist and archaeologist.

2. Unique formulations predominate in history as in anthropology. Generalizations are fluid, not strict laws; results stress significances rather than strict causal determinations.

The following may seem to contradict what has just been said above about holistic tendencies. Anthropologists' descriptions of particular cultures emphasize their distinctness from others, their peculiarities. What cultures share with one another tends to be dealt with more succinctly.

Most anthropologists are skeptical about "laws." Boas' early hopes of finding them were later given up, and the possibility denied. Historians and anthropologists are almost unanimous on this point.

3. Contextual coherence is a sign of good historiography, of good ethnology, and most markedly of good linguistic description, language being perhaps the most autonomous part of culture. "Coherence" is in terms of the whole and of the parts.

4. There exists a great world-wide web of permanent inventions, contacts, and spreads of culture components. The content of all civilizations and cultures is mostly of extraneous origin. More has seeped in from abroad than was devised at home. The alphabet, money, chess and cards, paper and printing are examples.

For many world-wide items of civilization we can now prove a single origin and spread. Some years ago Kroeber used the Greek word *Oikumenê*—the part of the inhabited world in which civilization existed—to denote the area of greatest concentration of this shared content of culture in Europe, Asia, and North Africa; exchange has gone on for thousands of years. Native Australia and America participated less. Even in the Old Stone Age long-range diffusions are evident.

5. These commonalties are not psychologically derivable (from "human nature," as used to be thought) but are products of historical events.

The time, place, and circumstances of the origin and further development of any institution, invention, or cultural form must be considered a legitimate and potentially soluble problem of inquiry through analytic comparison.

6. Civilizations are construable as precipitates of the events of history.

Inventions, customs, codes and values of civilization in an area are the residues of historic (and subliminally historic) events as these accumulate.

7. Culture is the common frontier of anthropology with historiography and its branches such as Sinology, Egyptology, etc. This holds especially for remote and ancient civilizations.

8. Anthropology is ready to help interweave all data on culture into a history of human culture; but it cannot adequately do so alone.

There is a vital need for professionally equipped experts in the various fields. China, the Islamic world, ancient Egypt, etc. have such experts. And as the desire to achieve the larger goal becomes widespread, the contacts of anthropology with these segments of scholarship will increase.

9. To achieve the larger goal is not an impossible task—biology serves as an encouraging example.

In two centuries biologists have worked out a coherent, reasonably reliable, and still growing history of life on earth ("evolution"). They have done this largely by trusting each other—by having common methods, a common front of attack though on many sectors. They have woven a million different species—each a biological "invention"—into a meaningful scheme and history.

True, the task is simpler for biologists, because biological evolution is irreversible: a branching tree, with all flow one way. In human culture innovations are intricately recombined. Similarity may be due to common origin or to secondary interinfluences often difficult to separate. On the other hand, historians of culture have the advantages of vast bodies of direct documentation such as biologists lack.

10. Essentially, the comparative study of civilizations is the history of all human cultures in their interrelations.

To many of us it seems desirable to have an over-all or macroview of this totality.

11. The model of such study is not in physics but in historiography and in natural history.

Philosophers have tended to set up mechanistic physics as the model for all science. This is unfortunate and belated. Hugh Miller and Hans Reichenbach both of the University of California, Los Angeles, are honorable exceptions.

12. The finding of pattern relations in context constitutes the essence of the historic approach.

The pattern relationship must be sought primarily in *natural* context, not in the artificial, isolated ("controlled") environment of experiment.

In fact, experiment is of course in the nature of things ordinarily impossible as regards the past, alike in the history of men, of civilizations, and of animal and plant development. This does not denigrate inquiry into these fields; it merely means that inquiry must be pursued by methods different from those of the laboratory.

The History of Civilization

There appear to be several ways of perceiving and presenting the history of civilization.

(a) One way selects and connects the culminating points of successive civilizations, on the basis of the influence they have had on later civilizations and ultimately on our own of here and now. Contributions of the past which are not actively effective today are very lightly sketched in or are wholly omitted. The story begins with the Stone Ages, goes on to the emergence of metals, cities, and writing in the Ancient Near East, then via Hebrews and Mycenaeans to Greeks, next of course Rome, then Mediaeval and Modern Europe. China and India hardly contribute to the dominant culture of today. Islam impinged from Mohammed to the Crusades, but since then can be virtually ignored, as can be pre-Mohammedan Arabia. Byzantium long seemed a wholly dead end of only antiquarian interest in the history of civilization; but since Russia has entered the competition for world dominance, Byzantine history reacquires a certain significance as an antecedent of Russia.

It is evident that this is a broadened variation of the "succession of empires" form of general history, which also snaked its way through history and geography by connecting the culminations.

This form of general history also finds a parallel in the popular story of biological evolution, with "ages" of culminating invertebrates, fishes, reptiles, mammals, and man.

(b) Biological evolution as viewed by and for biologists is less selective, and aims to give some account of and place for every novel phylum or originating line of development, irrespective of its dominance or success. Echinoderms and mammals receive treatment proportionate to the array of diversity they have achieved; among the chordates, the primitive or regressive lancelets, tunicates and lampreys get their modest but due place alongside the immensely more successful vertebrates, and mollusks are accorded consideration, instead of losing it, precisely because they embody a highly divergent sideline, though without important successors. The treatment, in fine, is strictly and totally comparative rather than selective.

We have as yet no successful histories of civilization on this plan, which would for instance not merge the account of Tibetan culture in that of India (or of China) but would emphasize also its original and its achieved distinctive features, such as a new form of Buddhism which showed its viability by successful export to Mongolia. Historians have been trained toward selectiveness; anthropologists have not been sufficiently trained in narrative. There have been reasonably systematic world ethnographies for more than a century, since Klemm, Waitz, and Prichard, but they have hardly risen above description.

The balanced comparative total history of human culture remains to be written. There is no reason why it should not be successfully accomplished, through a succession of individual tries, by scholars aware of the pitfalls of ethnocentricity and a too-great selectivity.

(c) A third procedure would be less a "history" than a "comparative anatomy" of recurrent characteristic crises or institutions or style phases viewed cross-culturally: revolutions (Brinton), feudalism (Coulborn), archaism (Flinders Petrie). This method compares "organs" rather than "organisms," aspects of cultures rather than total cultures.

The Historic Approach in Science Generally

This section differs from the preceding ones in having no specific reference either to "history" as a specific discipline (historiography) or to anthropology. It discusses "historicity" in the sciences generally: a historic approach, a diachronic aim.

1. Ordinary history in the conventional sense, history of notable human acts or events, narrated in the order in which they occurred, is perhaps the earliest body of organized knowledge. It originated fairly soon after the invention of writing in Mesopotamia, Egypt, and China, was taken over by other peoples as they learned to write, including the Hebrews, who gave it a theocratic instead of dynastic slant, and experienced a culmination in Athens of the fifth century B.C. in the still living histories of Herodotus, Thucydides, and Xenophon. These constitute the earliest corpus of organized human knowledge which remains alive and is still read for its intrinsic interest today.

Its subject matter of course is the doings of men, not the events or order of nature. It would be extreme to say that Greek fifth-century history—or the somewhat later history of Ssu-ma-chien—achieved everything that historians of today accomplish. But it accomplished astonishingly much; and its writers continue to be revered as masters today. These early great historians and their immediate Roman imitators are closer to their modern successors in what they achieved, than are ancient scholars and scientists in any other field of knowledge and scholarship.

2. Other branches of Greek "science," in the widest sense of the word, as for instance Sarton employs it, reached their peak development later than the Greek florescence of history. In the lifetime of Thucydides, Greek mathematics was still more than a century from achieving the completion of even its first stage, namely geometry under Euclid; astronomy and physics required two centuries to reach their apogee under Hipparchus and Archimedes; in other words, historiography, qualitative and diachronic, arrived at fundamental maturity earlier than did quantitative and synchronic natural science. This is a cardinal and really remarkable fact, especially in view of the subsequent career of total science.

It seems fair to construe ancient physics and mathematics as essentially synchronic. While they determined recurrent events, they found these occurring not in sequences but in an order which transcended sequence and therefore was essentially above time. True, it had become possible to predict certain future events; but this was precisely because their cycles of recurrence were by eternal law and therefore changeless and timeless.

3. After this, human *scientia* stood nearly still for almost exactly two thousand years, as regards its essential method. Historiography widened its scope but claimed no basically more advanced procedures. Mathematics, astronomy, and physics shone with Copernicus, Galileo, Descartes, and Newton, but their basic orientation was still toward eternal fixities into which time entered only as a measure of repetitive recurrence.

It was only about two hundred years ago that we find the first beginnings of an interest in long-range temporal and non-repetitive events of nature. It was the same eighteenth-century Laplace that completed the mechanistic understanding of our solar system, who also went beyond this in asking how this so regularly functioning system came about, and propounded an answer as to the origin in one version of the nebular hypothesis: Kant evolved another version; the answers are a classic example of the principle of the simultaneity of discoveries and inventions of fundamentally new ideas. At least, a new type of question was being asked about the solar system, and before long about our galaxy and the universe. The discovery of the enormously long orbits of some comets pushed thinking in the same direction. So did the penetration of more powerful telescopes. We ask today whether the universe is expanding or contracting—in which direction it is changing, instead of trying to delimit its changeless fixity. Astronomy has become recognized as a "historical science."

Other historical sciences of nature have developed without much in the way of ancient antecedents: geology, for instance, whose present foundations began to be laid in the late eighteenth century and took shape in the nineteenth.

Biology goes back in some measure to Aristotle, but as a wholly fixed order of life. The eighteenth century launched a systematic classification of living forms under Linnaeus, and then a beginning of physiology which led on into biochemistry; but both these still dealt with static or recurrent conditions. It was not until Darwin—just about a century ago—that the jam was broken, and life forms were seen to have had flow, origins and development, an evolution, and that biology was recognized as possessing a historical as well as a nomothetic aspect.

Still later, genetic biology began with the discovery of "laws of heredity." Yet less than sixty years have sufficed to reveal the extreme complexity of these laws and to shift prime interest from them to the mutations which alter the laws and bring change into the history of life.

It is plain that natural science has developed more diachronic concern, more of the longer historical approach in its interests and repertory, in the last two centuries than in the two millennia before. Instead of historical orientation being a sign of immaturity of development in science, we might almost affirm that natural sciences require a certain maturity before they *can* develop historical orientation.

4. Why should this be so?

One thinks first of Biblical orthodoxy. But Greek science was just as static as was Christian. And literalistic fundamentalism probably actually grew during the nineteenth century as it felt the tide rising around its Mosaicism, somewhat as the twentieth-century Dayton trials high-lighted its final protest.

More likely, religious dogma merely reinforced a deeper pervasive fear of flux as against fixity, fear of an unstable past and therefore unstable future replacing the comfort of eternal repetitiveness. Even the intellectual problems of a world forever spinning in its ordained place are simpler and easier than those of an embarcation on the boundless unknown. At any rate, the fixities and regularities were the first worked out, they were verifiable, and they came to seem very precious. By contrast, the historical approach in natural science involves fluidity, change, complexity, the continued facing of a penumbra of uncertainty.

5. Also contrastively, the historical approach in science presupposes a vast body of systematized knowledge to operate with. It is doubtful whether even the Greeks would have been interested in such a body of information, or have known how to organize it. The revolutions of the heavenly bodies are after all rather few, quite patent, and relatively simple to determine with surprising accuracy, once observations are patiently accumulated over a few generations, as is shown by Mesopotamian, Egyptian, and Mayan astronomy and calendry. The Greeks had observed fossil seashells on mountainsides, and rivers visibly building up their deltas. But it did not occur to them to attack the problems of mountain formation, of erosion, of tracing sequence by succession of strata, of comparing the strata of different regions. Most of the data resulting from inquiry into such problems would have seemed to them to be lacking in intellectual interest, to be merely informational and anecdotal: they did not integrate either with geometry or with virtue. Such would at any rate have been the attitude of Socrates and Plato. It was only the occasional Greek like Herodotus and Aristotle who was genuinely curious about natural phenomena in general. The civilization as a whole was incurious: it never developed Aristotle's beginnings either in comparative zoölogy or in comparative politics.

The historical interpretation of nature presupposes two conditions. The first is a willingness to deal with becoming as well as being, with flow as well as fixity. The second is the possession of, or the willingness to assemble, an adequately large and growing body of compared knowledge, of information in its natural context. Such a corpus is indispensable for understanding the history equally of the stellar universe, our earth, life upon it, or its human culture. Without such a series of corpuses, and a willingness to examine and organize each one comparatively, there can be no historic interpretation of nature on any of its levels; there can be only pseudohistoric guesses.

6. As regards civilizations or human culture, we have in hand a fair beginning of such a corpus. More data would help, but the need is primarily for more fruitful and reliable comparison of what is already known. There has really been very little attempt at basic classification of civilizations, either of their diachronic courses or of their synchronic anatomies, functions, and generic properties. There have been some intuitive stabs, exaggerations, identifications by formula. Even these have their value as first endeavors that may have to be largely rejected but which may enable later tries to lay securer foundations; and in that light they will be examined next time. But it is clear that most understanding of these matters is still unachieved. Yet there is no reason to fear that it will remain unachievable. In proportion as we recognize both the merits and the limitations of our predecessors, we are enabled to move beyond them.

12. The Personality of Anthropology

To DEFINE or characterize the personality or individuality of anthropology, I will start from a paradox.

When we compare anthropology and sociology, it is astonishing how alike they prove to be in their general assumptions and basic theory, and how diverse they yet are in most of what *de facto* they do or occupy themselves with.

Sociologists and anthropologists agree in dealing with sociocultural phenomena autonomously. Sociocultural data rest on biotic and individual psychic factors, of course, and are therefore limited by them; but they are not derivable or constructively explicable from them. The analysis and understanding of sociocultural phenomena must be made first of all in terms of sociocultural structure and process: "social facts," Durkheim called them; Spencer, "superorganic" effects; Tylor, "culture." As regards man, his societies always exist in association with a culture; his cultures, with a society. A particular study can abstract from the social aspects of a situation to investigate the cultural aspects; or the reverse; or it can deal with the interaction of the social and cultural aspects. This is common doctrine of the two sciences; and in contrast with what they share, it is really a minor matter that sociologists show a propensity to focus their interest on social data, structure, and process, but anthropologists on cultural.

Reprinted by permission from the Kroeber Anthropological Society *Papers*, No. 19 (Fall, 1958), 1–6.

In fact we can go farther. The basic assumptions and principles shared by sociology and anthropology are virtually the only *general* theory existing in that area which it has become customary to call "social science."

Economics, politics, jurisprudence obviously concern themselves with specific facets of society and culture instead of their totality. Psychology is of course basically oriented toward individuals, or *the* individual, much as is biology; social psychology represents a secondary extension, in the development of which sociology was about as important, at least in our own country, as was psychology itself. The classical economic theory was formulated earlier than sociocultural. This was possible because it applied to only one special part of the sociocultural totality: it was also a well-insulated model, whose effectiveness rested upon the assumption that economic phenomena could profitably be considered in a virtual vacuum; if motivations had now and then to be admitted, common-sense psychology was sufficient.

Not only do sociology and anthropology then essentially share their basic theory, but this theory is the only holistic one yet evolved for the sociocultural realm.

In view of this sharing of their basic concepts, it is remarkable how preponderantly sociology and anthropology do *not* share the areas which they work and the methods by which they work them.

Most conspicuous, of course, is the virtually total neglect by sociology of several of the fields which between them constitute probably the majority of the area operated in by anthropology.

These fields are: physical anthropology (a most unfortunate name, but this is not the occasion to try to revise it); archaeology and prehistory; linguistics, general, descriptive, and historical; culture history; primitive ethnology; and the folk ethnography of peasantry in civilized countries as it is pursued in Europe. Sociologists do not hesitate to use results obtained in these subdiciplines; but they rarely make intrinsic contributions to them, as all anthropologists do in one or more of the fields.

Now it is notable that with one exception—that of primitive

ethnography—all these fields are, however, shared by anthropologists with non-anthropologists. Physical anthropology of course is only a fragment of biology, and whether a worker is physical anthropologist, anatomist, or human geneticist is largely a matter of what he calls himself or of his job classification. Archaeology inevitably runs into art and classics—there even are notable departments named "Art and Archaeology," and our Archaeological Institute of America was founded and is run by classical scholars. Somewhat similarly, prehistory merges into protohistory and full history. More scholars have become general linguists coming from the various philologies than from anthropology. Culture history has been pursued also by historians and geographers, and some of the best has come from Sinologists. European folk ethnography is closest to what we call folklore, and in folklore students of English and other current languages of civilization are the more numerous. The result is that unless anthropologists are ethnographers, they share their specialty with collaborators in some natural science or in some humanity and are likely to be outnumbered by them.

What impulse is it that drives anthropologists as a group to participate in so many fields which are already being cultivated by others? It seems to be a two-prong impulse to apperceive and conceive at once empirically and holistically. We constitute one of the smaller learned professions, but we aim to take in perhaps more phenomenal territory than any other discipline. Our coverage must of necessity be somewhat thin. Yet it is rarely either vague or abstruse—we start with concrete facts which we sense to carry an interest, and we stick with them. Perhaps our coverage can fairly be called spotty; though without implication of being random, irrelevant, disconnected. If a whole is steadily envisaged, the relation of its fragments can be significant, provided the parts are specifically known and are specifically located within the totality. So the holistic urge is perhaps what is most characteristic of us.

This is balanced by a love of fact, an attachment to phenomena in themselves, to perceiving them through our own senses. This taproot we share with the humanities. And we also tend strongly here toward the natural history approach. Sociologists have called us "nature lovers" and "bird watchers," Steve Hart says; and from their angle, the epithets stick. There are anthropological museums of tangible objects, but no sociological ones. We are strong on photographs, films, and tapes that reproduce sights and sounds. We write chapters on art in ethnographies and sometimes offer courses in primitive art. How many sociologists would venture that, or even wish to venture it?

We insist on field work as an opportunity, a privilege, and a professional cachet. We want the face-to-face experience with our subjects. The anonymity of the sociological questionnaire seems to us bloodless, even though its specificity and quantification are obvious assets to which we cannot easily attain by our methods. When the Lynds went in person to study Middletown-Muncie, it was widely heralded as a taking-over of anthropological technique.

To return to the other prong of the bow, the holism, this seems expressed also in our inclination to historical and to comparative treatment. American sociology is certainly neither antihistorical nor anticomparative in principle; but it certainly is heavily interested in the here and now, in our own culture and social structure more often than in foreign, remote, or past ones. Sociology began with a marked ameliorative bent, and with concern for practical matters of utility. Anthropology commenced rather with an interest in the exotic and useless. We did not constitute our Society for Applied Anthropology until 1941. The "action research" of World War II was largely thrust upon us by government and military, and by many is remembered as a sort of spree of forced decision-making.

It is certainly significant that the sharing of anthropological fields is with the natural sciences and with the humanities. The only active overlap with any social science is that on theory with sociology. Specific primitive ethnography and most of the community studies in civilized societies continue to be done by anthropologists, quantifiable studies of problems in civilization by sociologists. The latter tend to define terms more sharply and problems more limitedly. They probably rank next to economists and psychologists in abundance of statistical treatment.

Balancing our virtual agreement on sociocultural theory, there exists, however, a strong drift in sociology to emphasize social structure and social action as compared with cultural product or pattern, and either to ignore the cultural accompaniments or to assume them as being somehow contained in or derivative from the social structure. Anthropologists, at any rate until recently, have contrariwise emphasized culture as their concern. To be sure they have made almost a fetish of kinship and have frequently given close attention to specific social aspects, ever since the initial days of Morgan and Bachofen. But they tend to look upon society as a part or domain of culture, on which one can specialize or not as one can specialize on religion or art or values, or again on subsistence, technology, and economics. Each procedure seems to give consistent results in the hands of those who follow it.

However, there is a point which no one seems yet to have thought quite through. Developmentally, evolutionistically, society far antedates and thus underlies culture, as shown by the existence of complex societies especially among insects, long before any culture existed. In man, who alone of all species substantially possesses culture, this invariably coëxists with society. In analytic study they are separable, and in practice one can focus on societies, or on cultures, or try to focus on the interrelations of the two. However, it remains conceptually unclear, at least to myself, how the sociologist can successfully treat culture as something in or derived from social structure, and the anthropologist can with equal success treat social structure as only a compartment or sector of culture. There is some legerdemain of words at work here, I feel, which my rational eye is not fast enough to perceive. I must admit I have found few colleagues who were seriously troubled by the contradiction that puzzles me.

I encounter a possibly related blocking of thought when I try to define "social anthropology" as a conscious movement or strand within total anthropology. It has emerged since my own maturity, as a successor to "functionalism," and the present generation of British social anthropologists have been trained by the "functionalists" Malinowski and Radcliffe-Brown. In Britain, where sociology is little recognized, social anthropologists stress the "social" aspect of their work and appear to accord primacy to social structure much as do American sociologists. At the same time they are obviously interested in cultures holistically, much as the rest of us are, and they are excellent ethnographers, as indeed Malinowski was when he did not let facile theorizing seduce him away from his superb descriptions of concrete culture functioning. But why the separatism, the limited circle?

In America social anthropology seems to have started with Lloyd Warner when he came back from Radcliffe-Brown in Australia. Warner is interested in the interactions of persons in society, especially our own, and perhaps most of all in social mobility. He uses cultural data skillfully to vivify his basically social-structural findings.

Perhaps the British are really still doing ethnography—reporting on culture—but are giving it additional *depth* by socializing it more than when Boas, Lowie, and I were doing field work. If so, the fact would take social anthropology out of the category of an exclusive cult, and would leave it as an endeavor at needed and vital enrichment of long-established cultural aims.

In that case "social anthropology" would resemble culture-and-personality, or personality-in-culture, which started out self-consciously as a revolutionizing new dimension of anthropology, but seems now to be essentially adding greater depth of personalization to the analysis of culture than was at first thought necessary, possible, or meet.

Since personalities are initially determined by their ancestry, it is highly relevant that anthropology was not a social science at all originally. Its father was natural science; its mother, aesthetically tinged humanities. Both parents want to attain reasoned and general conclusions; but they both also want to reach them by way of their senses. After a brief first childlike decade of outright speculation, anthropology settled down to starting directly from experienced phenomena, with a bare minimum of ready-made abstraction and theory, but with a glowing conviction that it was entering new territory and making discovery. Its discovery was the world of culture, an enormous product and a vast influence, with forms and patterns of its own, and a validating principle: relativity. There were far boundaries to this demesne, which included in its totality alike our own and the most remote and diverse human productivities. The vision was wide, charged, and stirring. It may perhaps fairly be called romantic: certainly, it emerged historically about at the point when aesthetic romanticism was intellectualizing. The pursuit of anthropology must have seemed strange to many people; but no one has ever called it an arid or a dismal science.

Now, maturity has stolen upon us. The times, and utilitarianism, have caught up with us, and we find ourselves classified and assigned to the social sciences. It is a dimmer atmosphere, with the smog of jargon sometimes hanging heavy. Generalizations no longer suffice; we are taught to worship Abstraction; sharp sensory outlines have melted into vague ones. As our daily bread, we invent hypotheses in order to test them, as we are told is the constant practice of the high tribe of physicists. If at times some of you, like myself, feel ill at ease in the house of social science, do not wonder; we are changelings therein; our true paternity lies elsewhere.

I do *not* end on a note of despondency; for the routes of fulfilment are many. It is well that with all their differences of habitus, of attitude, of building stone, sociology and anthropology have emerged with a substantially common basic theory. That should be an encouragement to both; and a rallying point to others.

13. Evolution, History, and Culture

THERE IS disproportion between Darwin's specific contribution to science—the origination and substantiation of the principle of natural selection—and the overwhelming effect which the establishment of this purely biological principle came to have on total science. There was evidently a particular historic concatenation in the world's thought which enabled Darwin's discovery to trigger consequences so great. This concatenation and its effects is my subject of inquiry.

In the first place, because Darwin's contribution was so essentially biological, we tend to forget how slow its complete absorption into total biology was, while the world around was being shaken by the revolution which the biological innovation induced.

It was indeed a revolution, against which orthodox religion promptly mobilized its full strength, the dissenting factions perhaps even more bitterly than the established and prosperous. The final offensive effort in the long retreat of orthodoxy came in the Scopes trial at Dayton in Tennessee sixty-six years after publication of the *Origin of Species*. There was of course no valid reason why the biological sphere should not always be autonomously ruled by biological decisions. Yet the minority of age of biological science had lasted so long that the guardianship and authority

---

Reprinted by permission from *Evolution after Darwin*, edited by Sol Tax (Chicago, University of Chicago Press, 1960), pp. 1-16.

of dogma over it had come to be accepted as almost perpetual and inherent.

Then there was the important fringing corona of rationalism, whose interest had largely shifted from God to man. So far as this element of opinion was also anticlerical, it tended to find comfort in the alarm with which organized religion viewed "Darwinism." On the other hand, so far as the intellectual element posited its values in specifically human qualities like spirituality or the categorical imperative, the evolutionary bridging between body and soul was quickly sensed as disconcerting. After all, Darwin in person took this inevitable step within twelve years with *The Descent of Man*, as remorseless a demonstration as it was a restrained one.

From outside, it probably looked as if all must be elation in the biological realm so suddenly freed from its immemorial dependent or colonial condition. But actually the going was rough, in spite of ardent patriot propagandists like Thomas Huxley and Haeckel. Sexual selection aroused doubts early; the nonfunctionality of organs still in the emergent stage was a troublesome problem; use and disuse as a contributing causal factor, which Darwin himself as well as Spencer continued to accept, was a rotten and treacherous prop. Above all, there was little systematic knowledge of heredity and variation, the two grand factors on which selection was to operate. It was obvious enough that heredity and variation existed, but only as averages or trends of masses of phenomena, evident as wholes, but unanalyzed and unmeasured.

This was still the situation when Mendel was rediscovered around the turn of the century. Overwhelmingly, biologists had been accepting evolution because there was nothing else for them to do; but they had not proved it to their own satisfaction. The developing science of genetics for a while contributed perhaps more new difficulties than new aids; as Huxley says ("The Emergence of Darwinism," pp. 1–21 in *Evolution after Darwin*. Vol. I: *The Evolution of Life*), it took time to reconcile the new fundamental principle of genetic discontinuity with the continuity of phenotypic evolution. The result is that the achievement of successful Neo-Darwinism barely antedates the battle of Dayton, after which reaction could no longer be mobilized.

As regards the grand over-all effect of Darwin's life and work on the world's thinking, it seems to me that he did more than anyone else to establish a historical approach as valid in science, and that the significance of this may be even greater, and perhaps will be more enduring, than what he accomplished for biology as such. This is what I had in mind when in opening I referred to what Darwin "triggered." He may have been mainly unconscious of this larger effect, though I doubt if he was wholly unconscious of it. At any rate, I now come to my central task, which is to consider how and why this triggering occurred. That in turn involves consideration of Darwin's place in general or total science. Under "general science" I would include any organization of knowledge and understanding based solely on naturalistic principles, irrespective of subject matter.

The Historical Approach to Science

Can human history, in the ordinary sense of the word as history is written, taught, and studied, be included in total science? I think it must be so included. It is recorded and sifted knowledge, always organized with reference to time and space, usually organized also with regard to significance, and as far as possible concerned with cause and effect, though admittedly only subjectively and fumblingly. The significances stressed may be predominantly moral, or again patriotic; they can also be enhanced by the manner of writing, which fact involves an aesthetic element. There are intellectual problems contained in the materials of historiography, ranging from considerations of human nature to those of progress and destiny; and the range of consideration can be very broad or intensively narrow. It is evident that the manners of doing historiography are varied and plastic, and its findings equally so. There is in it little of refined or special technique; and this condition is borne out by the fact that fairly competent history was being written both in China and on the Mediterranean between two and three thousand years ago. In the time since then, most or all other branches of science have been developed, refined, and enriched enormously, even though in jerks and starts and by no means continuously. In other words, the study of human history still operates by essentially primitive methods: it is our archives, libraries, decipherment of strange writings, and control of foreign languages, our footnote and reference techniques that have progressed in bulk and organization since Thucydides, rather than the interpretations made by historians. Historiographic research, almost alone, remains without systematic and "theoretic" results. Some would say that it is knowledge but not science because it remains on a concrete level and does not abstract.

On the other hand, historiography obviously deals with the description of events in the flow of time and operates with an ease and success that it took all the remaining branches of science a very long period of apprenticeship even to approximate. Darwin's is a household name not because housewives and householders are deeply and clearly concerned about natural selection, but because Darwin is the symbol and was in large measure the agent of natural science finally achieving the historic approach of evolution, of being willing and able to operate in biology without reservation or constraint in the dimension of time. In retrospect, it seems very difficult to realize that this achievement could have been mainly delayed until only a century ago. As a historian of sorts, I am impelled to reflect upon and analyze this anomaly of the intellectual history of our civilization, and in fact of the human species and its attribute of culture.

I am driven to begin with a hoary pair of opposites, the static and dynamic. It is a platitude, though a significant one, that static situations are generally easier to analyze and understand than dynamic ones. By definition, they exclude change; they do not involve the dimension of time; there are no events. In physics, statics preceded dynamics; in mathematics, geometry developed before algebra, and in teaching beginners, this order is still largely followed.

However, historical inquiry, though lacking any serious systematization of principles or generalizations, and therefore generally accounted as being on the most rudimentary and retarded level of science, is overwhelmingly dynamic: its subject matter is events, that is, changes!

This anomaly is evidently the result of its subject matter, which is the interactions of the most complicated and variable of units known to occur in nature—human beings—and these viewed preferably not quiescent and at rest (when historiography also slumbers) but in full and multiple interaction. The bigger the interpersonal and mass shocks and the greater their effects, the more significant and interesting does history become.

Now, not only are human beings inherently the most variable of natural units, but they have further developed a faculty of increasing their variance with originality, creatively and exponentially. The product of this exponentially varying faculty is what we have come to call human culture or civilization. It has the added scientific disadvantage of being extremely difficult to isolate from context and environment for manipulation into experiment and test. It is no wonder that having chosen such a tough, subtle, and refractory subject matter, historiography has remained literally primitive in its scientific method: as regards general theory, the more easily productive fields of research had been preëmpted by physicists, chemists, and biologists.

As a matter of fact, historians every so often leave off their prevalent narrative flow in order to hold a moment or brief period steady while they review the state of the institutions, economies, arts, manners, attitudes, and values, at the moment selected, in the country or area they are dealing with. They call such a treatment "topical." The examination is placed in time, but it is not diachronic internally. What further distinguishes such a topical discursus (or independent essay), is that the endlessly varying events of narrative history are now left out of consideration in favor of the pervasive regularities of human behavior in the period and area in question. In other words, description of institutions in the widest sense of that word, or, more generally, of "culture" or form of civilization, replaces the usual narrative of particular and unforeseeable doings and happenings. Essentially such topical treatments by historians are sociological or anthropological in their nature. In dealing with what is customary, predictable within its limits, and therefore regular, such topical history must certainly be included within the confines of natural science even by those who would deny such inclusion to merely narrative historiography.

In such a "topical" description of a culture, whether by a historian or an anthropologist, time does not enter because the "moment" chosen, even though it cover a century or two, is short enough for changes in it to remain unimportant relative to stable conditions persisting through it. If due consideration is given to the interrelation of the several aspects of the culture and society, one to another, the description will rise from the merely enumerative level to being functionally integrated; in other words, an over-all pattern is now being distinguished.

In short, there exists a kind of history, or spontaneous outgrowth of historiography, which by renouncing narration of the endless particularity of the primary data of human history, and confining its span to a virtual moment, attains to some of the generalization of natural science. This gain is achieved by foregoing a dynamic approach for a static one. The topic or moment of culture dealt with is viewed in equilibrium.

Pre-Darwinian Social Thought on Progress

This examination of historiography has been made because the concept of evolution which Darwin set off with such astonishing success is, in the larger sense, a historical concept: a process operating with change through time, and mainly irreversible and non-repetitive.

For the actual history of science, it must be significant that, in the half to three-quarter century preceding 1859, the notion of evolution was more widely held as applicable to social man than to animals and plants. This was certainly expressly true from Condorcet on. This may be so in part because the time span of man is so much briefer than that of most of nature. And yet man's evolution was early conceived as going on through the whole of his existence. In any event, the actual priority of a widespread conviction of human evolution, before much belief in the evolution of life was held, is undubitable.

This socioculturally oriented evolution of man's condition and achievement was viewed as progressive, and included the comparative value judgment of change for the better, of improvement. In fact it was probably based primarily on this value judgment, whereas Darwin basically argued only that species "originated," that is, life forms could change instead of being immutably fixed.

The time of Condorcet and his fellows and followers was too early for them to be properly describable by the modern term "social scientists"; but they were not natural scientists. The idea of progress may have originated with the discoveries and extensions of knowledge in the age of explorations that began in the fifteenth century. It was certainly connected with the Quarrel of Ancients and Moderns that arose in the seventeenth century as a result of the political and cultural florescence of France under Louis XIV, and from there spread through Europe, with the balance gradually inclining more and more in favor of the moderns, until in the eighteenth century the verdict crystallized as "Enlightenment," newly achieved. Condorcet was followed by Comte with his three stages, and in England by Spencer, who is reckoned as a pre-Darwinian evolutionist, though his naturalistic knowledge was second-hand and his system largely speculative even though sober.

It is presumably in this stream of social and philosophic thought that the idea of the permanent effect of use and disuse originated and was then injected into biological thinking as "inheritance of acquired characters"—a doctrine that Spencer invoked, Darwin refused to reject, and that died hard—Freud being the last great name to cling to it. In recent biology it is often called Lamarckism, though Lamarck himself used it to explain secondary evolutionary modifications or deviations from the immanent pattern or eternal configuration of the organic realm (G. G. Simpson, "The History of Life," pp. 117-180 in *Evolution after Darwin*. Vol. I: *The Evolution of Life*). Transmission of acquired characters of course actually does take place on the sociocultural level, and on a large scale. The phrase is a somewhat crude but largely sound description of the normal process of culture change and history. Culture does alter by use and disuse, much of it does accumulate, all culture is always acquired by learning. The mistake lay in the transfer and application of the idea to the genetically dominated realm of the organic.

Preconditions of Evolutionary Biology

As we look back to 1859, the wonder today is that Darwin's triggering could have been historically postponed as long as it was. There is not only his own hesitation of a score of years. It would seem that the geological evidence alone, still more as it was reënforced by the palaeontological, would have sufficed to force a break-through decades earlier. Religious dogma was an influence, but no longer the decisive one in nineteenth-century European science. It may be that it just comes harder for human beings, including scientists, to face a changing cosmos than a fixed one. Hellenic religion prescribed next to no dogma with which an evolutionary or diachronic way of thinking would have conflicted; yet Greek science also cheerfully confined itself to a fixed world.

As a matter of fact a review of the total history of science reveals very little real concern with a historical approach until after 1750, except of course for human historiography. Such a concern is therefore a late and rare phenomenon in the history of science.

However, to substantiate this finding it is necessary to distinguish two aspects within the dynamic approach: a microdynamic, which seeks for regularity within process, and a macrodynamic, which alone is wide open and genuinely historic in interest.

The phenomena of night and day, of the moon, of the year are characteristically short-range, dynamic, and repetitive. To transpose slightly, it might be said *Plus ça va vite, plus ça dure longtemps:* things spin and reel, but their order and result stay the same. The situation is dynamic indeed, but it is also dynamically fixed. Even the Copernican overturn, Kepler's laws, Galileo, and Newton did not alter this basic outlook. The first break was speculative, when Laplace and then Kant tried to imagine how the solar system had come about and devised a nebular hypothesis in explanation of its history. An empirically historical science of astronomy had to await more powerful telescopes, photography, and the spectroscope—in short, a vast increase of knowledge due to technological progress.

The earth sciences of geology and paleontology confront obvious phenomena that seem to us, who have acquired historical orientation, to demand historical interpretation—the superposition of strata, for instance, and comparison of similar fossil-bearing strata in different parts of the earth. Yet as long as information on these matters was scant, spotty, irregular, there was little sure sequence of conditions to be got out of the data. So guesses as to the primacy of this or that favored set of processes—neptunic, volcanic, diluvial, catastrophic—simple "origin" hypotheses—were advanced and argued. It was only as systematized and coherent knowledge—contextual knowledge—grew, that arbitrary lunges at seizing a basic process barehanded were crowded out by the growing mass of information which almost enforced a system of interpretation by its own mass. The geological frame of factual knowledge and process appears to have been substantially ready for macrodynamic and evolutionary understanding some decades before Darwin—and an understanding not too different from the present-day one. I can only guess tentatively what prevented the consummation. Perhaps no amount of piling on of technical evidence alone could suffice. Some great public event was needed that both touched dogma and released dramatic human affects. This quality perhaps was supplied by Darwin's dealing with organisms which by implication included mankind and so stimulated human interest more than any merely geologic process could have. If this suggestion is inadequate, those whose knowledge of the history of geology is fuller can amend it.

Within biological science, Linnaeus was a necessary precondition to Darwin; especially so, Linnaeus' system as modified into the "natural" system of classification of life forms, based on investigation into total structure. In fundamental theory, Cuvier was the antithesis of Darwin; but his "types," converted into genetic phyla, still hold largely today, underneath the accumulated mass of reënforcing knowledge.

In celestial, terrestrial, and organic science alike, the first beginnings toward use of what became a historic approach occurred about the mid-eighteenth century, and achieved acknowledgment about mid-nineteenth, centering around Darwin, who made the first conscious and directed break-through. It had by then become clear that all natural phenomena had a potential history if they could be placed in designable space and time.

The latter half of the eighteenth century also saw the foundation of scientific chemistry, which however developed into a fundamental and ahistoric science in increasingly close association with physics. The causes for the lateness of chemistry can therefore not well be the same as for the historic sciences, but they may be allied. I hazard that the nature of the phenomena of chemistry is such, as compared to those amenable to the approach by physics, as to require a larger organized corpus of knowledge before sound interpretation can be effected.

An Exception: Philology

A lone exception to the rule of pre-Darwinian absence of macrodynamic approach appears in philology. In the late 1780's Sir William Jones recognized the common origin and diverging descent of the Indo-European languages—an insight which grouped species of idioms into genera and genera into a family, resulting in a genuine phylogeny, perhaps the first in any field of knowledge. Strictly speaking, Jones' finding was preceded by some recognitions of similarities within Indo-European subdivisions and within some non-Indo-European groups of languages. But these tended to be construed rather as variations or "corruptions" of one extant language, whereas the large gap in time and space between Sanskrit and the earliest recorded languages of Europe shifted construal of the Indo-European situation into one of descent of daughter languages from a reconstructed common mother tongue.

From the point of view of general science, several significances characterize this recognition of Indo-European descent. First, the recognition was derived empirically, forced by the evidence, not speculative. Second, it was not concerned with social thought about progress. Third, it originated in the humanities, and dealt with language which is a segment of culture, although a clearly defined concept of culture was not elaborated until about two generations later. Fourth, the principle of inferring common descent from parallel similarity of form and structure proved applicable to other groups of languages, because specific patterns of linguistic change were found to possess significant regularity even though their specific causation remained unknown.

It would seem now that this priority of the genetic scheme of Indo-European descent was in some degree the consequence of the particular nature of language. Comparison has not yet provided equally consistent demonstration of lines of descent or regularity of change for the remainder of culture. Nor has any discovery been made which explains causally the mechanism of linguistic change in a manner analogous to the light which the science of genetics has thrown on hereditary conservation and change in biological evolution. The early discovery of linguistic phylogeny thus remains an unexplained anomaly or sport in the history of science. But though puzzling, it is indubitable and remarkable, and its precise *raison d'être* will no doubt be discerned before long.

I can only suggest a favoring condition: the existence of a

well-established and thorough organization of relevant knowledge, in the shape of accurate grammars and lexica of Greek, Latin, and the principal mediaeval and modern vernaculars of Europe. This accurately classified corpus of data would necessarily add much weight to the significance of similarities discernible on comparison with an older and remote Asian language such as Sanskrit. Jones had available a well-worked-out philological taxonomy, as Darwin had available the post-Linnaean cumulative taxonomy of plants and animals.

Darwin's Influence on Anthropology

When the revolution so long planned and still deferred by Darwin finally came, most of the sciences immediately underlying biology were affected powerfully and rapidly. But the overlying sciences dealing with man were much less stimulated or influenced by him. Historiography and economics were long almost unaffected, as was concrete sociology. Theoretical sociology must be excepted—but then it had had its own pre-Darwinian progress theory. Psychology was still so unextricated from philosophy as to be too immature for much influencing. Philosophy itself was surprisingly little affected. It did increasingly drift away from its traditional problems into becoming the commentator and appraiser of natural science; but to date it has recognized very little in science beyond what can be conformed straitly to the model of physics.

The one science of man whose course reacted sharply to the impact of Darwin was anthropology, which even in its formative days had always contained a definite "natural history" interest—as it still insists on retaining an avowedly biological beachhead—and which was perhaps the least encumbered by normative and ameliorative aims.

In the 1840's it looked as if the several strands of anthropology might coördinate themselves as "ethnology." Societies were formed under that name in Paris, London, and New York. In Germany, since 1843, Klemm was assiduously describing assembled ethnographic data under the title of *Cultur-geschichte* and *Culturwissenschaft,* and he was certainly dealing with cultural phenomena though he seems to have been unable to formulate a clear-cut concept of culture. In England, this was the period of Prichard and Latham and their natural history approach. Data were growing, though theory was still weak. Morgan's first book, the descriptive *League of the Iroquois* (1851) belongs in this stream, and is distinctive chiefly in being based mainly on direct inquiries among the people whose culture is depicted.

Such was the sort of hesitant, unspectacular drift which characterized what was to become anthropology, for some fifteen years before the *Origin of Species* was published. The effect of this event was tremendous: a crop of founding fathers of a science of anthropology sprang up within two years, and within the dozen years to *The Descent of Man* many of the basic books of "Classical Evolutionary Anthropology"—as it later came to be called—had appeared. Here is the list:

1861: Bachofen, *The Matriarchate (Mutterrecht)*
1861: Maine, *Ancient Law*
1864: Fustel de Coulanges, *The Ancient City*
1865: McLennan, *Primitive Marriage*
1865: Tylor, *Researches into the Early History of Mankind*
1870: Lubbock, *Origin of Civilization*
1871: Morgan, *Systems of Consanguinity*
1871: Tylor, *Primitive Culture*

The principal additions that might be made to this early cluster would be Morgan's *Ancient Society* in 1877 and Tylor's *Anthropology* of 1881.

What had these books, half of them by jurists and only one (Lubbock's) by a banker-naturalist, to do with Darwin's natural selection as a mechanism of biological change? Nothing whatever, directly. But their authors were evidently stimulated by the idea of evolution to which Darwin had given a foundation. It is of interest that Lubbock, although professionally a banker, was also a competent naturalist. He drew inferences from original observations and experiments on social insects, which have stood up better than his speculative interpretations of cultural origins. If it was now revealed that there had been great changes in the forms and structures of animals and plants, there were likely to have been great alterations also in man's status and condition, in his institutions, customs, and mode of life. What Darwin had done for life in general—giving it a history—they were proposing to do for human culture.

Limitations of Early Anthropology

There were two reasons why these first anthropologists could not achieve a solid success similar to that of Darwin—why, in fact, the course of the evolution of culture still remains much less certainly ascertained than that of life. The first of these reasons is that Darwin inherited a highly accurate, solid, and comprehensive classification of animals and plants which had developed by systematic coöperation among biologists since Linnaeus, more than a century before. As against this, the would-be anthropologists had a helter-skelter miscellany of travelers' tales and missionaries' accounts, from which obtruded some picturesque features: the couvade, matriliny, divine kings sacrificed, houses of snow—somewhat like elephants' trunks and armadillos' armor in pre-Linnaean natural history. An added difficulty became clear only gradually: the family tree which outlines the history of life is throughout a one-way affair: once two life forms have diverged a very little, they cannot ever reassimilate or merge again. But culture, without genes or genotypes, and floating through and out from phenotypes, is protean in its sources. It can differentiate and reintegrate; it can assimilate or be assimilated by other culture or exist alongside; a new item can develop from within a society or from others without.

What could these early anthropologists do to develop an evolutionary history of man's culture overnight? They more or less knew the end of the story—the human successes of their day.

They could imagine a beginning, which, if there had been any notable evolution, would have had to be quite different, and which they called "the origin." The word was fashionable: Darwin himself wrote the *Origin of Species* instead of the *Evolution of Organisms*, as Huxley points out. Naturally, the beginning of the evolution of culture and custom was posited as having been as different as possible from achieved cultures: it was the contrastive opposite, or the condition of cultureless animals. Then, all that lay between was filled in by plausible speculation, more or less propped by such available evidences as were favorable. It was much the same process of thought as that by which the Greeks at the threshold of their philosophy-science explained the origin of the world: the "first" was water—no, fire, for everything changes—no, it was air—better yet, mind—or wait, nothing had ever grown, for logic breaks down before motion. Like these early Greeks, the early anthropologists did not actually know anything of the course of actual events nor of the processes which had shaped their course. There was really not much they could do but conjecture plausibly. It is in general a sign of ignorance when we profess to seek or know the origin of any group of phenomena without knowing something of its history: the true origin, being farthest from us, is likely to be the last discovered. Probably we tend most to manufacture origins when we have least actual knowledge of post-origin developments. Ignorance of history breeds myth.

Later Phases of Anthropology

However, something did emerge from the tremendous interest that was stimulated in a group of intelligent men such as the evolutionistic anthropologists were. Their answers were mostly of little worth, because they asked the wrong questions; but they founded a science. They did this by occupying a phenomenal area which rested on the organic but extended beyond it, and which therefore had a degree of autonomy, including processes of its own. A central field became defined in these first dozen years:

it was that of institutions and custom. Tylor first called this subject matter by a general name, "civilization," in the subtitle of his 1865 book, and Lubbock followed him. By 1871, Tylor shifted to the less implication-laden "culture" which he took over from Klemm, defined clearly, and used to delimit his field. He also got away from the dominating concern with social-political-legal institutions which preoccupied most of his contemporaries, and rounded his culture off by giving due attention in their own right to religion, technology, and even language. Tylor accepted autogenic development, but also recognized external cultural influence; and he was the first to try to ascertain by empirical counts which features of culture intercorrelated or "adhered" to one another. With his stock-taking booklet of 1881, he even crystallized the name "anthropology" for the field of natural science he had staked out.

True, Tylor was also influenced by the century-old stream of social thought concerned with improvement and progress. But this influence was superadded to his natural science thinking—somewhat as Darwin accepted use and disuse effects—without unduly warping his empiricism and curiosity.

A second phase of "classic evolutionistic anthropology" began around 1890 and centered around Frazer, who has influenced the emotional thinking of more non-anthropological readers—including Freud—than any other anthropologist, but who is virtually outside the current of the present-day science. Frazer was a classical scholar by training, and his active following was mainly classical, literary, and British: Andrew Lang, Gilbert Murray, Jane Harrison, Robert Graves; Hartland, Crowley, and Briffault also belong. This group was perhaps more concerned than the first with explanations by endogenous or spontaneous psychology than with generic human evolution.

It is clear that these so-called evolutionistic anthropological movements stemmed from the commotion that Darwin produced in opening up possibilities of more than static interpretation, but that they were scarcely influenced by Darwin's specific work or thought, nor, if they had tried to interpret the history of human culture, would they have had the organized data to do it with. Later anthropologists have had to begin all over again. We have by now learned several things: not to compare ethnocentrically; not to use data torn out of context, nor loose fragments of structure; that good description must be in terms of the described society's and culture's own nature, structure, and function, not in terms of any merely logical scheme—just as in biology; that structure cannot be analyzed too searchingly; that it is wise to lean heavily on the findings of archaeology because incomplete as these are they are always solider than reconstructive conjectures.

The Need for Classification

All in all, during the past half-century, anthropologists have been most interested in pursuing microdynamic work, in analyzing out the structure, and the changes of structure and function, of relatively small societies and cultures, within spans mostly of less than a lifetime, the communities involved being mostly subnational of the order of tribes, villages, or localized minorities. This restriction of scope satisfies the need to work holistically which most anthropologists feel, and yet it makes possible the rather reliable determination of the sociocultural mechanisms involved. But it also leads to spotty and diverse results which are slow in adding up to larger findings, whether of mechanism or of the general course of growth.

Macrodynamic inquiry into culture is being consciously or directly pursued by few anthropologists and by few historians. It is being kept in vision by some; much more than that is probably not feasible at present. The organized corpus of comparable knowledge is as yet too scant and discontinuous: it is much as if Julian Huxley and George Gaylord Simpson had tried to do their present work two hundred years ago. True, there is a rather large total aggregate of cultural description extant; but very few works share the same specific aim. One stresses psychology, another the unique particularities of its culture; one attempts to test a hypothesis of greater or less range, another follows a conventional pattern of topics; some accounts are oversensitive to cultural style, others insensitive, and so on. The situation is made more difficult by the fact that anthropologists still tend to value personal expertise, technical virtuosity, cleverness in novelty, and do not yet clearly recognize the fundamental value of the humble but indispensable task of classifying—that is, structuring —our body of knowledge, as biologists did begin to recognize it two hundred years ago.

I am not speaking in distress. I believe the need will be felt— is being felt; and once it is recognized, classificatory organization may begin suddenly to be supplied on a scale now undreamed of. Historiographers may participate—in fact may well take the leading part. The profession of historiography has only to gain by the recent movement, now well under way, to include historians of so-called exotic areas, of science, of the arts, which were formerly left wholly to Sinologists, scientists, critics, art theorists, and such. This in addition to economic and social history, and "history of ideas," which are of longer standing as admitted specialties within history. The time may even be reasonably near when general or universal history will be attempted by scholars for scholars, as in the days of Voltaire and Herder, but with far greater resources, and perhaps coöperatively rather than through the idiosyncratic genius of some Toynbee or Barnes working single-handed. (It is a curious aberration of the moment that most of our present-day general histories are aimed specifically at eighteen-year-olds who have just entered the university and who in America at least are as good as untrained in seeing significance in any historical phenomena.) Purely political history, and national history, will always continue, because they will always be wanted. But there is no reason why historians should not also try gradually to take over the whole history of man, which when thus generalized inevitably becomes the history of human culture.

Huxley has clearly recognized both the break in mechanism between organic and cultural evolution (he sometimes calls the latter "noetic" or "psychosocial," with neither of which terms do I quarrel), and at the same time the fact that cultural development has largely taken over the determination of what will happen on this planet both to life and to culture. ("Man's Place and Role in Nature," pp. 79–97 of *The Unity of Knowledge*, ed. Lewis Leary, 1955; also, "Evolution, Cultural and Biological," pp. 3–25, in *Yearbook of Anthropology—1955*, ed. Wm. L. Thomas, Jr. The respects in which biological and cultural evolution are importantly alike and importantly unlike are skillfully summarized by Huxley in two paragraphs at the turn of pp. 24 to 25 in the second article.) When Huxley first presented these views to a group of anthropologists at the Wenner-Gren Foundation about 1951, he aroused mainly unrest and opposition: I do not know precisely why, unless the audience mistakenly feared that ethnocentrism and challenge to the autonomy of culture were rearing their heads. Similarly, when in my 1948 *Anthropology* I revived the old problem of progress in culture, and cited four ways at least in which progress seems substantiable by objective evidence, the reception in the profession was cool if not negative: Redfield alone, so far as I know, has spoken up in general agreement. The prevalent attitude was evident again in the International Congress at Philadelphia in 1956 when Russian visitors raised the issue. I confess I am puzzled by the negativism; I hardly like to attribute it to a fear of words—to a dread that because Spencer's and Morgan's nineteenth-century "progress" was ethnocentrically slanted, any acceptance of progress is ethnocentric. To be sure, a property of accumulativeness widely and loosely attributed to culture is connected with the idea of progress; but we have lately began to distinguish differences in the degree and kind of accumulation in different cultural fields, and there is every reason to think that this problem too can be handled evidentially without loose thinking.

Summary

I have tried to show some of what Darwin in 1859 released in effects outside of biology. Through an unusual combination of circumstances, of which religious dogma was one but only one, biology had remained confined in a static framework for most of the century before, while geology had very nearly broken through to recognition of a long-range history of the earth's crust, in all but formal declaration; and social thought, though speculative and unorganized as to data, had accepted progressive evolution as a principle, though still within a short-range time span. Astronomy in widening its compass beyond the cyclic recurrences within the solar system had embarked both upon a historic approach and a long-term one. Recognition of diachronic change in biology was therefore overdue; so that when Darwin combined the genius of his insight with masterful use of the long structural-taxonomic accumulation, the principle of natural selection broke through to an explosively revolutionary recognition in biology; and this revolution was immediately extended to the underlying earth sciences and the overlying sciences of man and culture, especially anthropology, which, rooting in the natural sciences, was directly affected as historiography and sociology were not.

While anthropology acquired direction and cohesion as a field of science in the dozen years following 1859, its first findings were largely misdirected and sterile because it possessed no corpus of classified knowledge comparable to that of biology, and had to fall back mainly on speculation. In this it went further astray by short-circuiting a genuinely historical, gradualistic approach into an illusorily diachronic quest for ultimate origin. Tylor, in extricating the concept of culture as the distinctive subject matter of anthropology, and by a certain sobriety and balance of his speculations, which left room for historical considerations, salvaged the science, which toward 1900 began to steer into the courses it has since followed. However, anthropologists as a group have been unnecessarily slow in recognizing the necessity of organizing the body of their knowledge into a systematically comparable form, as observational geology and biology have done so thoroughly and fruitfully.

Both the microdynamic and the macrodynamic approach are

justified and profitable in the field of culture, and in the end ought to supplement each other. The macrodynamic emphasizes the time factor more and deals with longer time spans. It thus connects naturally and easily with biological evolution on the one hand and with human historiography on the other. Since biologists have come to recognize that with the evolution of specific human faculties cultural factors have been increasingly superimposed on selective genetic ones, and bid fair to be the prime determinants of terrestrial evolution from now on, it would seem that anthropologists should reciprocate in coöperating with efforts to see evolution as one continuing course, though with a cardinal change in the course. When it becomes recognized that culture is in one sense the endlessly complex and unordered behavior of men seen ordered through a lens of long-enough focus, historiography and culture study can join hands instead of viewing each other across a gulf. We shall then be in position to realize such continuities as exist between the evolution of life forms, the manifestations of culture, the past behavior of men, and perhaps their present behavior in mass.

14. On Human Nature

AMONG CULTURELESS or virtually cultureless animals, it is relatively easy to describe their characteristic behavior, just because it is practically unimpinged on by the highly variable factor of culture. A large component of their behavior is genetically founded, and, since physical environment tends to be stable and long-term, the effects of this environment have mostly been incorporated in the genetic constitution of the species through selection. The influence of organic environment or ecology has also been at least partly absorbed into the congenital make-up. The remainder of the organic environment is obviously, in a state of non-domestication, the principal factor which makes for individual learning.

The result is that we know pretty well the characteristic behavior patterns of bovines or felines, of chipmunks, porpoises, or elephants, of wrens and loons, of snakes and frogs. While reports by amateurs on the behavior of animals may often inject anthropomorphizing and dubious motivation, a mass of thoroughly reliable observation by zoölogists is also available. The behavior is the externally directed functioning corresponding to the animals' bodily structure. It bears obvious resemblance, greater or less, to human behavior and conditions, and is therefore construable—provisionally at least—in "psychological" terms. In some cases we can now infer which parts of the behavior are con-

---

Reprinted by permission from *Southwestern Journal of Anthropology*, Vol. II, No. 3 (Autumn, 1955), 195–204.

genital and which individually learned. In others, the discrimination can be made by sufficient observation, properly directed; or if necessary, by test. We have therefore in hand or within reach a considerable body of objective knowledge on the behavioral "nature" of various animals: the essential and constant qualitative patterns of the psychological activity of many very different species.

By contrast with all subhuman species, in man the behavioral picture is enormously complicated by his possessing culture. Culture is of course based on a genetic endowment—indeed presumably a very special cerebral genetic endowment. But, viewed operatively, culture is supergenetic. It is acquired by learning from other individuals of the species, and is practiced and somewhat modified by each member of the human race individually; and his modifications enter into the continuum or joint product which is passed on to subsequent individuals. The chief mechanism which makes communication of human culture possible, and thereby makes culture possible, is the faculty of symbolization and speech. This faculty is hereditary: all normal human beings possess it to an adequate degree; other species possess it, at most only to a rudimentary degree. It is certainly the most fruitful in effects of all the specific characteristics of man; and it is difficult not to believe that the faculty must be the result of a genetic mutation or group of mutations.

Culture, including speech and symbol or idea systems, is individually acquired—"learned" by each individual from the other individuals he associates with. As these groups of associates or societies are spread in many parts and environments all over the earth, and as these have each had a more or less separate and different history, they show much diversity. This notorious plasticity or variability of human culture is due precisely to the fact that its content and forms, its substance, are non-genetic, and are therefore exempt from the overwhelmingly repetitive and preservative influence of heredity. The customs—which viewed systematically are the culture—of human societies often differ drastically; and their languages differ radically and totally—as much perhaps as orders, classes, or even phyla of animals, if such a comparison may be made by way of illustration. Yet in their organic morphology, the most divergent human societies are only races within the confines of one zoölogic species.

Owing to the largeness of this highly variable component of culture in the make-up of human behavior, it is evident that "human nature" is a much less steadily uniform thing, and much harder to characterize, than gorilla or elephant or tiger nature. Its hereditary features carry an enormous overlay of variable features due to culture. In fact, social psychologists and some sociologists often say that there is no human nature as such— only Chinese, Italian, Hottentot, etc. human nature. This seemingly absurd statement of course means only that generic human nature is so molded or distorted or reshaped by Chinese culture in China and by Italian in Italy, that it nowhere occurs or is given as such; and this is a warning to naïve fellow-psychologists that they must not assume they are dealing with pan-human psychology when they are describing contemporary American behavior, no matter how refined their tests or statisticized their method.

Actually, of course, though it can not possibly anywhere be uncovered in its purity, original or pure human nature exists as a theoretically separable and essentially constant component in the Chinese, Italian, and the hundreds of other ethnic or social groups, which are fusion products of genetic, individual-accidental, and sociocultural influences.

While psychologists at least aim at universals, as they pervade individuals, the first focus of anthropologists is on specific features of groups, as that of historians is on specific events or on particular and even unique conditions. Anthropologists expect to deal primarily with human nature as it is expressed in the dress of particular cultures, and are not disturbed by its particularity as psychologists would be. As a matter of fact, for several decades they have been very little troubled by what generic human nature might be, because they had come to realize that it was far more constant than actual, culture-determined human nature; so much so that they would not be far in error, in the present state of precision or imprecision of their methods, if they simply assumed, provisionally, that generic human nature was constant. At least they could assume it as averaging about constant for races and societies, though not for individuals; but then individuals are not their first professional concern.

Incidentally, historians, who are less theory-conscious even than anthropologists, have made and do *de facto* make the same assumption, whether they are aware of it or not, that human nature runs alike in all larger groups of men.

The earlier anthropologists, it is true—those who promulgated broad evolutionistic speculations beginning in the decade of the *Origin of Species,* and until as late as 1895–1915—far from discounting human nature as a factor profitably ignored, built on it. They were still, as in the early phases of many sciences, confident that they were discovering unconditional universals, and progressive ones. And what was there better to derive their universals from than human nature? It was the basis and mainspring of all human action, individual and social; so institutions and beliefs just spontaneously grew out of it. Consequently beliefs and institutions in one place and another, at one time or another, tended to show a strong similarity. It was through accidents that they differed, and incidentally; in their important aspects they were similar—must be related because they all flowed out of human nature. Time and again Frazer in establishing a relationship or a sequence says: "What is more natural than that this should happen" or "that they did so and so." Frazer indeed strongly savored exotic practices and beliefs; but it was as seasoning of the steady monotony of a diet of universals that were an emanation of our nature.

Those easy, golden years of just dipping into the human nature of common experience to make anthropological science about primitives and origins are long since over. They were succeeded by the era of criticism and cultural relativism. As a result, it became apparent that human nature had not been defined; that it would be very difficult to characterize in all the Protean forms which it assumed; that it evidently was basically rather uniform; and that it could therefore be cancelled out of our operations as a constant.

Now this period in turn is drawing to a close, and basic human nature is once more being felt as an existent. Bidney brings it into his *Theoretical Anthropology* of 1953; Spiro into a 1954 *American Anthropologist* article. It is a subject that is again being talked about by anthropologists; and it is clear that we cannot permanently ignore the basic genetic part of our psychology.

This essay then attempts to suggest some ways in which the problem of human nature may be grappled with.

It will, however, clarify this objective if we first eliminate some procedures that seem unfruitful.

First, we shall not learn to understand better what human nature is if we try to begin with a formal verbal definition of what is meant by human nature. Useful definitions come at the end of inquiry.

Second, inquiry must be systematic, utilizing the known results of previous scientific inquiry. This rules out any verbally more elaborate restatements of the commonplaces of common knowledge and common sense. It is not that these are without truth. But so do all proverbs contain truth, and yet scientific inquiry does not start from or operate with proverbs, be they overt or pedantically disguised.

Third, we may leave aside consideration of the "common denominators" of culture which have been several times proposed, exemplified, and even listed by anthropologists. Again, it is not that they are untrue; but they seem useless: no one has been able to develop the approach. I suspect the reason for this sterility to be that the emphasizing of common denominators is at bottom an endeavor to define human nature from culture, to deduce it from culture; which is open to objection equal to that of deriving culture from human nature. The two procedures might be described as inverse forms of reductionism.

The same holds for the "universal pattern" of culture, that seed lightly tossed out by Wissler that has never germinated.

Once more, the concept is not untrue; but an enumerative table of contents, while useful in its place, is not a productive tool for research.

Finally, we shall rule out "needs," including needs that appear under new names. Basically, they also are commonplaces of common knowledge. If elaborated, they are usually psychological restatements of cultural behavior.

There may be several approaches toward the problem of defining human nature, but I discern only two with any specificity. There are abundant data available for both; but the data need more systematic examination from the angle of our particular problem. Before we attain new results it may be necessary to assemble additional facts, or to recheck or reinterpret some of those on hand. But the first step would seem to be a comprehensive and systematic shaking down, from our point of view, of what there is in hand.

The first approach is intraspecific and cultural; the second, comparative and biological.

The approach through culture is simple. It would aim to delimit the perimeters of historic human culture, as established by the most extreme expressions yet found in particular cultures, of the various activities and qualities of culture. It is not to be expected that this delimitation would *per se* lead to any profoundly novel discoveries. It would be an organized stock taking, a systematic review from one angle. But the limits of human culture, both normal limits and extreme ones, are presumably set mainly if not wholly by the normal and extreme limits of congenital human nature. And such a delimitation of the expressions of human nature would at least be a first step toward defining our problem by including as well as excluding those phenomena presumably most relevant to human nature. It might be at least the beginning of an escape from the mishmash of common and inexact knowledge, common and dilettante speculation, and unrealized hangovers from religious and ethical systems, that make up our present thinking or talking about human nature.

An exemplification of "most extreme expressions" is human

sacrifice as practiced by the ancient Mexicans; or frequency of cannibalism among certain Polynesians and Melanesians. In completeness, intensity, and variety of asceticism I presume the inhabitants of India have gone farthest, as they certainly have in intensity, variety, and nonresidualness of hierarchical grouping in castes, and—along with the Tibetans—in institutionalized polyandry. In the realm of thought, first place would presumably also go to India both for philosophical pessimism and for love of classification on its own account. India is of course mentioned only for convenience of identification: it is the cultural manifestation that is the relevant material, not the place or people.

The Japanese forty-seven ronins would perhaps serve as an extreme of institutionalized loyalty. For pervasive cleanliness, neatness, order, finish, and restrictive elimination of physical superfluities, the Japanese would again come strongly into consideration; for going without artifacts, tools, and property, the Australian natives.

These examples may suffice to make my meaning clear. I have deliberately avoided citing any from Western civilization for fear of bias in perspective and evaluation where there is participation.

Even brief consideration of this topic seems to indicate that certain cultures, such as the Chinese, will be represented but rarely at the perimeter of pan-human extremity; others of equal size and weight of achievement, such as the Indian, repeatedly. The theoretical preëminence accorded the sage and priest over the ruler; the propensity toward the abstract, the priority allowed the conceptual over the sensory, the addiction to exaggeration and absolutes, are further cases in point from India. Followed up systematically, this side line of frequency evaluation should result in a rating of cultures on a scale of centering respectively well in the interior or toward the rim of the total range of human culture (and therefore human nature, presumably); or perhaps of nearness to different segments of the perimeter. This is of course not part of the problem of human nature as such, but it might be a by-product of the proposed line of investigation. But even as an avowed distraction this side issue serves to show how much more readily problems loom into sight when a field is viewed for a time from one consistent angle than when it is viewed indeterminately from several.

Incidentally, if this suggested side line proved productive, it seems that the differential placing of disparate cultures within the perimeter of total human culture and total human nature might also contribute to the definition and characterization of the "modal personality" of these cultures.

At any rate, total human culture viewed historically and comparatively—cross-culturally is the modern word—obviously must essentially coincide with human nature from which it grows; and its perimeter being therefore the perimeter of human nature, this definable coincidence suggests itself as an opportune toe hold from which to start further inquiry into human nature. I do not know where else in the range of the two aspects, than at the periphery, we can allege any point-for-point correspondence of their phenomena.

It is true that potential human nature almost certainly has a slightly wider range than the sum total of known culture expressions. The perimeter of recorded culture would therefore fall within that of the potential nature. But—one thing at a time; and it is unprofitable to think too much about what extensions or revisions of understanding the future may or may not bring.

It will be seen that the proposal is opposite to the method of Frazer and the former cultural evolutionists. Basically, they "explained"—actually, derived—certain of the more or less known phenomena of culture from the more immediately but less definitely known nature of man. I am proposing to start from the limits of known culture in the hope of finding somewhat better understanding of the undifferentiated magma of human psychic constitution.

The second approach would be a somewhat analogous inventory and methodical survey, among subhuman animals, of behavior patterns similar to or anticipatory of human cultural behavior patterns. This survey would be comparative between man and other animals; and between definitely culturally expressed patterns and predominantly congenital or individually learned patterns. These last two ingredients, the congenital (genetic) and the individually learned, should of course be distinguished whenever possible. But the distinction is not always easy at present; and when it cannot be made, the two could still be legitimately and perhaps profitably compared jointly with human culture—which is also learned and which also expresses, however variably, a congenital constitution, but which is acquired socially and symbolically.

For instance, it is widely maintained that an element of play or playfulness enters into human and therefore cultural aesthetic, intellectual, and perhaps religious activities. A sound and critical review of the nature and range of play in the animal kingdom as well as its absences, based only on sound biological data and interpretation, would supply a firmer foundation for our understanding of the "value segment" of human culture. It might even react back on biological interpretation.

The diversity of play behavior, as between phyla, classes, and even orders, is astonishing. It may be questioned whether any invertebrates play except as part of mating. The same may hold for the cold-blooded vertebrates; but scraps of exception would be most interesting. Warm-blooded mammals play mostly in youth, but warm-blooded birds never in youth. Even adult courtship play in birds tends toward intensity and seriousness. Nonsexual play is largely confined to a few families, such as crows and magpies and parrots.

Among mammals there are enormous differences. Insectivores and rodents play little; seals and whales possibly most of all. Primates vary—compare baboons and chimpanzees. If they play, it seems to be with accompaniment of unusual affect. Carnivores on the whole play more than herbivores; but there are contraries, such as the elephant on one side, and weasels and minks on the other. Some carnivores play until almost old age: raccoons and otters especially. The corresponding raptorial birds are playless, except for a few courtship flights.

There are many purely biological problems unsolved in this

area, especially as regards correlates of greater or less playfulness: size, diet, medium inhabited, protection and sustenance provided the young, and so forth.

This extraordinary organic and phylogenetic diversity has a striking analogue in the diversity and plasticity of those sectors of culture supposedly embodying expressions or sublimations of play impulses—the "value segment" of culture already mentioned. This may be mere coincidence; but it also suggests that systematized comparison might be fruitful—even on both sides of the line that separates the organic from the organic-plus.

It seems unnecessary at this stage to do more than enumerate some of the further topics that would be relevant.

The now notorious pecking-order and the whole realm of interindividual dominance suggest much in human social and political institutions.

The societal aspects of animal life are of course of primary importance because human societies are a precondition of human cultures. Moreover socialization is one human property that has been developed to a definitely higher degree and greater integration among subhuman bees, ants, and termites—which possess only exceedingly rudimentary traces of culture. It is probably significant that this inverse weighting occurs among the arthropods, a phylum very different from our own. There is excellent literature both on the social insects and on animal aggregations and societies in general, but it has not been adequately exploited by sociocultural studies.

The "schooling" of fishes (and birds in flight, etc.) is related to sociality but with special emphasis on kinaesthetic phenomena, and has obvious counterparts in culture and human social psychology.

Behavior related to ownership is most developed on the subhuman level with reference to space—the individual "territoriality" of many birds and some mammals and fishes. Much but not all of it is related to nesting, breeding, brooding, and nurture of the young. Certainly territorial ownership is far more widely spread, intense, and functionally significant in the subhuman area than all other kinds of ownership. Linton may therefore have been right in suggesting that human concern for property is an outgrowth of sense of territoriality. Curiously, the nonhuman primates seem to manifest rather little attachment to either places or objects.

Possessiveness toward objects has a very spotty subhuman occurrence—the presenting and stealing of pebbles by penguins, the thefts of shiny objects by crows and magpies, the hoarding of almost anything unusual by packrats, etc. Most warm-blooded species and even families seem to lack such behavior altogether; and so do probably all cold-blooded animals. When the trait does occur, its functional relevance seems weak, as if it were a selectively non-significant spill-over or "perversion" or residue from mating, breeding, home-building or food-storing patterns. It might also represent something like congenital aesthetic appreciativeness.

Home building ranges all the way from automatic secretions remaining adherent to the invertebrate body, through spun covers, cases, or webs, to elaborate constructions of extrasomatic materials by some birds and beavers. The structures may be individual or social; their function, protection of the individual or the offspring or the group. There is no close correlation with degree of total advancement: ants chiefly burrow or excavate, termites build with excretions, bees with secretions, some wasps with gathered mud or masticated cellulose. Most fish are homeless, some merely wave out a hollow or clearing for their young, but the subfish lampreys carry stones to their spawning place. Among mammals, rodents often both burrow and assemble bedding as well as storing food; carnivores may burrow; ungulates generally do nothing at all and are homeless; a few primates make gestures toward a nest of half-broken or bent branches. The prevalence of nest building among non-running birds is obviously associated with holding the eggs together during brooding and the fledglings during feeding, as well as with protection. As might be expected, nest building and a sense of territoriality show a strong correlation.

Nests and structures of extrasomatic materials are of course artifacts. Beyond "housing," however, artifacts are definitely rare on the subhuman level; and so is gathering or storage of anything else than food. There are a few cases of extrasomatic uses of "tools," such as wasps tamping with pebbles, finches holding broken-off thorns to spear insects in crevices, monkeys picking up and hurling missiles. A systematic and critical evaluation of these few cases of subcultural tools might be illuminating. So would be a comparative listing of all materials, both somatic and extrasomatic, utilized extrasomatically.

Finally there are the two important fields of dance, rhythmic play, song, noise for its own sake—in short, the field of the arts in culture—and of "communication" in the wider sense—signals, sentinels, "teaching," etc. Here the findings of the von Frisch group on bee communications are outstanding and hold hope both of more results to come and of extension to other families and orders. The imitative song and speech of parrots, mynahs, mockingbirds, etc. presumably participate in both "art" and "communication," and have a further relevance of their own in that the feature of copying makes them cases of learning from the outset. If these birds learn from members of their own species as readily as from individuals of other species, as is likely but seems not proved, we have indubitable tradition at work; and therewith culture, at least of a kind. I say "of a kind" because it serves no apparent survival function, direct or indirect, but seems a matter of random amusement, playful exercise, and fitful by-products. Could it be that human culture had its first origins in analogous trivialities, and only gradually developed its seriousness and major potentialities? If not, what is the philosophic and genetic relation of the aimless and sterile "culture" of these tradition-imitating bird species to our culture? The questions are cited as illustrations of the sort of problems that the comparative subhuman inventory suggested might raise or even answer.

Similarly stimulating might be a list of behaviors that occur universally in human societies and cultures but seem universally lacking in subhuman species. Such would be: knowledge of death, concern with the future, the incest restriction, religion, extrasomatic visual art, verbal or muscular expressions of humor. Some of these might have to be modified or withdrawn, but others would presumably be added. As the inventory consolidated and grew it might well suggest new and more precise perspectives on what factors subhuman organic evolution and human cultural evolution possessed in common and differentially.

I keep referring to inventory, review, stock taking because I believe there is a vast body of observations, a large proportion of them critical and sound, of natural history type in the fullest scientific sense of that term, which tend to seem largely of marginal significance to most biologists as they pursue their daily work, and which anthropologists are to an even greater extent too preoccupied to utilize. In fact, the segment of anthropologists that have entered the profession from the social science side are for the most part profoundly ignorant of this class of phenomena.

I am not advocating experiment, which is difficult and too easily lets its own technique overshadow results. The value of experiment, which isolates a situation from its context in nature, is at critical points *after* these have been determined. Psychologists with rats in mazes presumably know the critical points in their problems, which I take to be theoretical and definitional, not intrinsically comparative and certainly not historical. The series of problems to which my foregoing suggestions refer are broadly historical, being concerned with evolution—the relation of cultural history to organic history. No doubt there are critical points in this field which can ultimately be clinched by experiment—von Frisch and Lorenz have demonstrated this—but the first need is for sifting of the accumulated observations to sharpen the focus on what is critical. What I have done in the preceding pages is to try to suggest some of the considerations which might guide such sifting.

That absorption of the data is the first requisite is something I feel certain of. Knowledge, factual knowledge, descriptive knowledge of form and of behavior, is what Darwin accumulated for twenty years after he found the concept of natural selection; and it enabled him in a few months to write *The Origin of*

Species and establish evolution in the stream of modern thought.

I should love to participate in the adventure that I envisage and have outlined; but I must pass on the opportunity to younger bodies.

www.ingramcontent.com/pod-product-compliance
Lightning Source LLC
Chambersburg PA
CBHW021705230426
43668CB00008B/726